TABLE OF CONTENTS

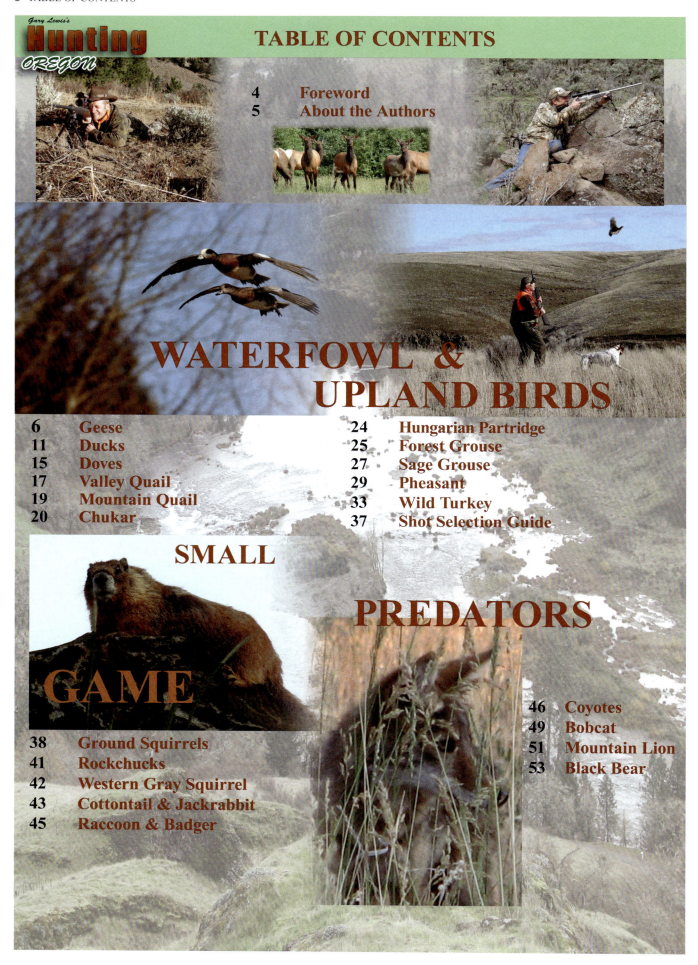

- 4 Foreword
- 5 About the Authors

WATERFOWL & UPLAND BIRDS

- 6 Geese
- 11 Ducks
- 15 Doves
- 17 Valley Quail
- 19 Mountain Quail
- 20 Chukar
- 24 Hungarian Partridge
- 25 Forest Grouse
- 27 Sage Grouse
- 29 Pheasant
- 33 Wild Turkey
- 37 Shot Selection Guide

SMALL GAME

- 38 Ground Squirrels
- 41 Rockchucks
- 42 Western Gray Squirrel
- 43 Cottontail & Jackrabbit
- 45 Raccoon & Badger

PREDATORS

- 46 Coyotes
- 49 Bobcat
- 51 Mountain Lion
- 53 Black Bear

TABLE OF CONTENTS

BIG GAME

59	Blacktail Deer
65	Mule Deer
72	Eastern Whitetail Deer
74	Columbia Whitetail Deer
76	Pronghorn Antelope
80	Rocky Mountain Elk
84	Roosevelt Elk
88	Bighorn Sheep
90	Rocky Mountain Goats
92	Feral Swine

WHERE TO HUNT

94	Where To Hunt
95	Map of Western Units
96	Map of Eastern Units

SKILLS & SAFETY

107	Still Hunting
109	Hunter Safety
112	Map, Compass & GPS
114	Survival
115	Shed Antler Hunting

EQUIPMENT

97	Knives
98	Rifles & Cartridges
101	Bowhunting
102	Muzzleloaders
103	Shotguns & Wingshooting
104	Optics

BEFORE & AFTER THE HUNT

116	Taxidermy
119	Meat Care
121	Outfitters
123	Wild Game Cooking
126	Passing It On
127	Appendix
128	Index of Advertisers

Gary Lewis's Hunting OREGON

Authors
Gary Lewis
Scott Haugen
Duane Dungannon

Publisher
Gary Lewis Outdoors

Editors
Larry McGlocklin
Merrilee Lewis

Interior Design & Layout
Chris Smith
Jennifer Lewis

Print Production
The Lynx Group, Inc.

Advertising
Brian Davis

Contributing Photographers
Gary Lewis
Eric Hansen
Scott Haugen
Duane Dungannon
Bill Truxal
Chris Smith
Calvin Halladay
John McFarland III
Dave Rein

About the Cover
Cover Image: Hunting chukar in north central Oregon
Inset image: Ken Klock on the ridge at sunset
Cover Design by Chris Smith

Gary Lewis Outdoors
P.O. Box 1364
Bend, Oregon 97701
www.GaryLewisOutdoors.com

Reproduction, in whole or in part, including advertising, is expressly forbidden without prior permission in writing from the publisher. In the event of errors in the publication, the sole responsibility of Gary Lewis Outdoors will be to correct such errors in a succeeding edition of the publication. Such correction is in lieu of any other remedy. Gary Lewis Outdoors expressly disclaims all other liability for loss or incidental or consequential damage whether arising from negligence, contract, or other cause to any party for errors in publishing. All submittals of photos, slides, artwork, etc. were handled with care, however the publisher assumes no responsibility for them. Although all efforts have been made to assure accuracy of content submitted by advertisers and writers, Gary Lewis Outdoors, its principals and associates are not held liable for errors or omissions.

Foreword

Checkered flannel and the smooth cycling of well-used rifle actions, the blued steel and wood, the hushed voices and the headlights that cut through the dark. These are the things we remember.

This edition of *Hunting Oregon* continues the tradition we started when Sun Publishing launched the title in 1999. We take a look at Oregon hunting from the Columbia to the California border, from the breaks of the Snake River and the Owyhee canyons to the breakers of the Pacific. In this edition, we feature all-new chapters and full color photography from Oregon's own Scott Haugen, Duane Dungannon, Eric Hansen, John McFarland III and Bill Truxal and more.

This book is presented in sections, starting with waterfowl and upland birds, small game and predators and chapters on hunting mule deer, blacktails, elk, bighorn sheep and mountain goats. In each chapter are hints to help a hunter locate hunting areas and game. We give helpful information on habitat and suggest specific regions to hunt.

There are chapters on archery hunting, muzzleloaders, rifles and shotguns. We tell you how to sight-in for big game hunts and how to hire an outfitter. We discuss hunter safety, survival and finding your way in the woods and the desert.

We have provided advertisers with an opportunity to tell of their products and services (see page 128 for an Advertiser Index). With information on resorts, hotels, outfitters, preserves, dog trainers and manufacturers, you will find this invaluable in planning your adventures. We are grateful to the businesses that supported this book and who have allowed us to bring you this high-quality publication at an affordable price.

Oregon has some of the best elk herds in the country, more bears than almost any other state, thriving turkey populations, four subspecies of deer and challenging bird hunts against spectacular backdrops. Take this book wherever you go and enjoy hunting Oregon.

Good Hunting,

Gary Lewis

Gary Lewis, Author

About the Authors

Gary Lewis

Gary Lewis is an outdoor writer, speaker, photographer and television host who makes his home in Central Oregon. He has hunted and fished in six countries and across the United States. Born and raised in the Pacific Northwest, he has been walking forest trails and running rivers for as long as he can remember. He is a past President of the Northwest Outdoor Writers Association (NOWA) and was recently presented with NOWA's Enos Bradner Award.

Lewis is a columnist for The *Bend Bulletin*, a Contributing Editor for *Successful Hunter* magazine a humor columnist for *Bear Hunting* magazine and a regular contributor for many other magazines and newspapers. His stories have appeared in *Sports Afield, Rifle, Successful Hunter, African Sporting Gazette, Boating Sportsman, Traditional Bowhunter, Mule Deer, African Hunter, Cascades East, Northwest Fly Fishing, Washington-Oregon Game & Fish, Oregon Hunter, Hunting the West, Salmon Trout Steelheader, Wheelin' Sportsmen* and more.

He has authored or contributed to eleven books and three DVDs. Five of his books have won NOWA's Excellence in Craft awards and he has received numerous awards for his newspaper columns and magazine articles.

Scott Haugen

Prior to entering into the outdoor industry full-time, Scott Haugen taught science for 12 years. With a Masters Degree in education, a bachelors in science/biology, and lifelong outdoor experience, Haugen is uniquely qualified to share what he knows and continues to learn. Since hanging up his teacher's hat, he's appeared on more than 250 television shows, penned over 1,300 magazine articles and written several books – with new titles always in the works.

Haugen also conducts several seminars each year at sportshows, club events, churches, men's groups and more. He also makes numerous guest appearances on radio broadcasts around the country.

Scott Haugen, his wife Tiffany and their two sons, Braxton and Kazden, live at the foot of Oregon's Cascade Range, in western Oregon. While Scott pursues a television and writing career, Tiffany is the creator of numerous, highly popular, cookbooks.

Scott Haugen spends more than 200 days a year in the field, hunting, fishing, scouting and photographing wildlife. He wouldn't have it any other way.

Duane Dungannon

Duane Dungannon has been the editor and publisher of *Oregon Hunter* magazine since 1992. An Oregon native, he has hunted extensively throughout the state. Since serving an internship at *Field and Stream* in 1987, he has been a regular freelance writer with credits that include *Field and Stream, Petersen's Hunting, Game and Fish Publications, Mule Deer, Northwest Sportsman* and *Oregon Hunter*.

DEDICATION

In Memoriam
Ed Park
Outdoor Writer
1930 - 2008

GEESE

Take 'em!

Geese gabbled in the pre-dawn dark as we loaded our decoys and blinds into the layout boats. Wearing insulated chest waders, we slipped into the water and splashed through a field of flooded barley, sending ripples across the knee-deep water.

It had been warm and clear for wintertime and there was already the hint of new growth showing on the ground. Following the

Afternoon flight patterns are different from morning routes. If you're hunting all day, gather the decoys and reset them before the birds start flying again.

light from our headlamps, we pushed back the night. Darren Roe led the way to a crescent-shaped hump of land as the first hint of morning showed in the eastern sky.

Darren Roe and Gary Lewis bagged these specks from a flock that fell for the charms of the plastic impostors.

"We'll set up here," Darren whispered. "Yesterday this is where I found all the birds. Thousands of them. I watched them with binoculars and put them to bed at dark."

We tore stalks of grass and weeds to give dimension to our camouflage. Darren and Mike turned the decoys into the warm wind blowing from the south. Pat, John and Roger set up our blinds.

Yesterday the geese were eating the green barley shoots and their webbed tracks were still visible in the mud. Six hunters and a Chesapeake retriever named Gus crawled into blinds and waited.

Damp barley stalks and standing water stood fermenting in the unseasonably warm January weather. The water looked like amber ale. Through the doors of my blind, I saw birds on the horizon. Here, mallards raced low over the fields. There, an eagle hunted above the marsh. Strings of swans rippled across the sky, the morning sun flashing on their wings.

The calls of honkers were all around us, in the wetlands to our right, in the roosting area to our left. They drifted across the sky, sometimes inspecting our decoys as Darren and Mike gave speech to our plastic flock.

We used the mountains as references to point out the birds to each other, hunching down inside the blind as they drew near. "Eleven o'clock. Low. Birds coming at us from the gap. Eight of them on the left." We called to them and they talked to each other, dropping for a look, sometimes coming in, sometimes wheeling around us and heading away toward the wetlands across the valley.

Two came from the north, dropping to the decoys, dropping, dropping, cupping their wings. Within range now for Pat and John. "Take 'em," Darren said, and the birds flared. Pat and John turned and fired, connecting on both birds, splashing them down in the water behind us.

Gus strained at his tether, quivering. Mike released him and Gus burst from his blind to retrieve the first bird, then returned for the second. More birds were on the way. We scrambled for our blinds and Mike tucked Gus into his hide again. The Chesapeake's yellow eyes followed each flock as they passed overhead, then turned to watch us again when the geese were gone.

For several hours we saw few geese. John snored. I watched spiders climb up the stalks of grass and drop inside my blind. The floating decoys turned lazy circles on their tethers. Rain fell. We changed our set to coincide with the afternoon flight and settled in again to wait.

The western Canada goose is the only goose that nests in Oregon and can be found in the state throughout the year. In the fall and winter you may see snow goose, Ross, greater white fronted (specklebellies) and Black Brant.

All that counts is what's coming over the horizon. The beat

Early Hunt Targets Resident Canada Geese

If you want geese and you want them on dry land, in warm weather, plan a September hunt.
The only goose that nests in Oregon is the western Canada goose. The Canada goose population increased dramatically through the 1980s and 1990s. Annual springtime counts put adult Canada goose numbers at 51,000 birds. Special September seasons target these resident birds before other waterfowl hunts get underway in October.

A big flock of geese can have quite an impact on agricultural operations. The highest incidence of damage occurs on croplands in the Willamette Valley, the Columbia Basin, and in and around Roseburg, Ontario and Bend.

Brad Bales, a waterfowl biologist with the Department of Fish and Wildlife, recommends hunters prospect for geese in the bigger river systems, like the Snake River, along the Oregon-Idaho border and in southwest Oregon on the Rogue and Umpqua systems. "We've seen substantial increases in southwest Oregon," Bales said.

Look for croplands adjacent to canals, ponds, lakes and rivers. Scout private land feeding areas before the season starts. Geese feel most comfortable in harvested fields because the food is scattered and there are no standing crops to conceal sharp-toothed predators. Note where and when you see the birds, then secure permission well ahead of time.

Most hunters opt to ambush the birds in the field with grainfield patterned ground blinds in a large set of decoys.

The northwest Oregon September Canada goose season takes in all of Clatsop, Columbia, Multnomah, Clackamas, Washington, Tillamook, Yamhill, Marion, Polk, Benton, Lincoln, Linn and Lane counties, with the exception of some national wildlife refuges and state parks.

Those portions of Curry, Coos and Douglas counties east of Highway 101 and all of Jackson, Josephine counties and all eastern Oregon counties, except Klamath, are governed under a separate season. Bag limits are more generous in southwest Oregon.

In the September goose season, the taking of white-fronted, Aleutian and cackling Canada geese is prohibited. Bag and possession limits are liberal so check the Oregon Game Bird Regulations for exact details.

Goose hunters need a hunting license with the Harvest Information Program (HIP) and the Oregon Waterfowl Validation. Hunters aged 16 and older are required to have a Federal waterfowl stamp in their possession as well. Steel or non-toxic shot are required when hunting waterfowl.

Private Land Access

Because of the nature of this damage control hunt, hunting is only allowed on private lands. Secure permission prior to the season. Any public lands or waters owned or controlled by any county, state or federal agency are closed to hunting in this special season. Goose hunters must have, in addition to a HIP-validated hunting license, a Federal Waterfowl Stamp and a resident Waterfowl Validation. See the Oregon Game Bird Regulations.

FIELD DRESSING WATERFOWL

AFTER TAKING WATERFOWL IN OREGON, A FEATHERED HEAD OR WING MUST BE LEFT ATTACHED TO THE BIRD WHILE IN THE FIELD OR TRAVELING HOME.

of the wings, the direction of the wind and the feel of the wood against your cheek, and the thump against your shoulder.

"Here they come. Low over the marsh," Darren whispered. We craned our necks to peer over the tops of the blinds behind us. Three of them, coming fast. "Now."

Our guns came to our shoulders. Darren led the first bird by six feet, tumbling it. A second one splashed down in the water. The third sailed on. And Gus went back to work.

At the end of it, I had two geese to broil with butter, lemon juice, and pepper. With them I carried the memory of drumming wings and a renewed appreciation for the order in nature. What is better than taking life-giving, delicious meat – wild and free in its natural habitat? It's pure, it's organic. It's high protein with no fat, no cholesterol, and no added hormones.

As I cleaned the birds and put the meat on ice, I knew I would always remember those minutes before first light, the breath of the wind in my face, the patter of raindrops on the dark water, the way the cut barley bent with the breeze and the whispered anticipation of honking geese against a paling sky. This is more than meat on the table, it is the connection with nature that no one can deny when the groceries come from nature's bounty.

SCOUTING

Canada geese can often be found in agricultural areas interwoven with waterways. Cut grainfields allow them to graze, safe from predators.

Scouting, prior to the hunt, is essential. If you'll be traveling, a local connection can pay dividends on your hunting day. Note what time birds are seen in which fields and be there with your decoys the next day. Permission, when sought prior to the season, may gain you access to private lands. And large flocks of strategically-placed decoys with good calling will bring geese within shotgun range.

ON DECOYING There's no better place to learn the art and science of decoying geese than in the field. The day before you take to the marsh with shotgun and camo, hunt with your binoculars from the seat of your truck. Scout your hunting area and figure out what fields the geese are using and where they choose to feed.

In the pre-dawn light, put out as many decoys as you can. The more decoys you have, the better. Darren Roe regularly employs 75 or more. There's a strategy he builds into every single set and it's a challenge to see how to fool them once again into that final approach. "Their wings are cupped, their feet are down. Decoying is an art form," he says.

"Always make the spread look like the birds were the day before in the field. Of course have the wind at your back in your blind." Approaching birds will always set their wings to land into the wind.

Leave holes in the set (landing zones) close to your blind to give the geese a target on their approach.

"Put your furthest decoy away from you no more than

The Specklebelly

Not as big as the Canada goose, greater white-fronted geese tip the scales at about six pounds. They stretch the tape between 26 and 34 inches from the pink, spatula-shaped bill to the tip of their banded, fan-shaped tail. They have a wingspan of 53 to 62 inches. In flight, they move like Canada geese in a steady, direct manner with rapid beats of their long, pointed wings. The call is a distinctive bark that sounds like a laughing 'kla-ha' or 'kla-hah-luk' or a'wah-wah-wah.'

Also called specklebellies or specks, this bird gets its nickname for the scalloped, or black-speckled belly of the adult goose. Up top, they have an understated beauty with a plain brown head, and a white forehead. Their wings are dun-colored and their tails are dark green, black and orange.

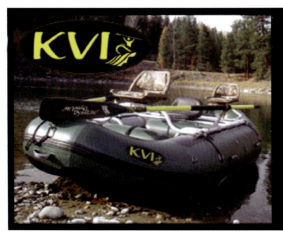

Kootenai Valley Inflatables
Introducing the "B-Series"

~ Superior Maneuverability   ~ Lightweight
~ Competitive Pricing   ~ Durable

www.KVIRAFTS.com

254 Lime Creek Lane   getwet@frontiernet.net
Troy, MT 59935   406.295.5001

30 yards. Birds have a tendency to land 10 yards away from your furthest decoy." Put a hunter nearby, Roe recommends. "You need someone on the fringe of your set so that your furthest shot will be no more than 25 yards."

Good decoys matter. Later in the season, the geese grow skeptical of their bogus plastic brethren. Darren mixes a blend of silhouettes and magnums in with his standard sizes.

Snow geese in the marsh at Dairy, Oregon.

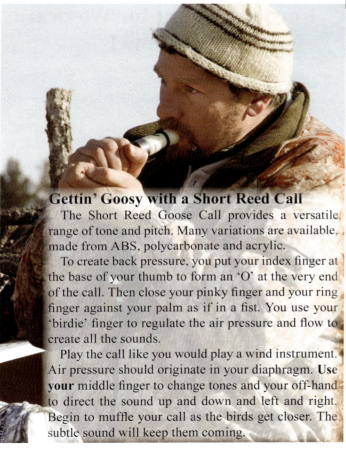

Gettin' Goosy with a Short Reed Call

The Short Reed Goose Call provides a versatile range of tone and pitch. Many variations are available, made from ABS, polycarbonate and acrylic.

To create back pressure, you put your index finger at the base of your thumb to form an 'O' at the very end of the call. Then close your pinky finger and your ring finger against your palm as if in a fist. You use your 'birdie' finger to regulate the air pressure and flow to create all the sounds.

Play the call like you would play a wind instrument. Air pressure should originate in your diaphragm. **Use your** middle finger to change tones and your off-hand to direct the sound up and down and left and right. Begin to muffle your call as the birds get closer. The subtle sound will keep them coming.

CALLING To be an effective caller you have to read the birds. Then talk to them as they circle your set. Roe believes that once you've called in a few flocks, you'll begin to figure out what kind of sounds the geese want to hear.

To start, everyone should learn the basics clucks and moans that make their calling sound goosy.

If you're new to the goose hunting game, whatever call you buy, spend some time listening to or watching the instructional tape and whatever other tapes you can find. Pay particular attention to the sounds that the callers make, when they make them, and why.

But calling is not always as important as your spread. The quality of the decoys matters. And how well you hide in the field matters.

Local birds have been hearing gunfire since September and the out-of-towners have been working their way south, encountering camo-clad hunters all along the way. And that's all part of the challenge calling us back to the marsh.

There's little that can compare to the thrill of watching a flock of geese on their final approach into the decoys, their wings cupped for landing. For a moment, time stands still, save for the thunder of the wings and the pounding of your heart.

On the Wings of Spring

We joined the hunt in progress a few miles outside of Klamath Falls. Brad Douglas parked the Expedition a quarter mile away. A field of white decoys shimmered in the afternoon sun. On the horizon, white snow goose wings winked against the sky, and a mass of birds

Bird Hunting + Fly Fishing = Excellent X 2
Ducks Geese Quail Grouse Steelhead Rainbows

OCTOBER — MARCH combo trips available
HUNT Private Property or Tulelake & Lower Klamath Wildlife Refuges.
FISH the Klamath, Wood, Rogue, Williamson or Umpqua Rivers.

call: **541.884.3825**
www.fishandhuntoregon.com

Matt Carey (right) and son Parker with the harvest from a cold day of goose hunting near Sisters.

seemed to lift out of the marsh, then tip and descend over the faux flock.

A single goose tumbled and then another and two hundred geese beat higher. Then we heard the shots on the wind.

We crossed the field as the hunters stepped from their coffin blinds to pick up their geese. Outfitter Darren Roe sent Georgie to retrieve a goose from the river. Kurt Ploetz had already bagged his limit. I took his place while he began to plan dinner.

There were birds on the horizon again. We shut the doors and peered at the sky through the straw. Before us, five dozen Dave Smith specklebelly decoys turned on their stakes and ten dozen snow geese dekes – full-bodies, shells and socks – rippled with the wind.

Sixty geese winged low over the river behind us, then tipped and wheeled, feet down on their final approach. "Take 'em," Darren shouted. The 20-gauge Benelli thumped and a Ross goose folded in front of me. To my right, Darren and the others found their targets.

SPRING (ALMOST) GOOSE HUNTING In the Klamath Basin, they're calling this the spring goose season, but technically, it's a late-winter hunt, focused on snow geese, Ross and the greater white-fronted goose. From late February into the second week of March, Oregon Department of Fish and Wildlife biologists use hunters to shift crop damage pressure from private croplands to the refuges in the Klamath Basin.

In the fall, white geese and white-fronted geese wend their way south to winter in California, New Mexico, Texas and Louisiana. In January, they start their way back north and many birds stop off in the Klamath Basin for two months or so.

"There are 300,000 excess white-fronted geese above management objective for the basin," Roe said. Not to mention the snow geese.

"The farmers' fields are just starting to greenup and get their new growth and the birds hit it and just keep grinding it down and the crops don't get a chance," Roe said. "These birds are feeding on anything from winter wheat to alfalfa and orchard grass hay. All that protein is important to their northern migration, but there is a lot of protein on the refuge."

Game managers are trying to encourage the birds to stay on the refuge. With one day left in the season, it seemed the geese needed more encouragement.

Encouragement for Wayward Waterfowl

At five in the morning, we headed east to Dairy. When Darren switched off the engine, we could hear thousands of geese jabbering in the dark. We set the decoys – specks to the right side and snows on the left, with a big 'landing zone' in the middle, then worked the next two hours breaking ice to give the birds open water.

For the first several hours skeins of white geese and specks drifted across the sky, too high to shoot. Time and again, specks or snows set their wings to drop in then wheeled out without giving us a shot. At lunchtime, we uprooted the snow geese socks which might have seemed suspect without a breeze to animate them.

Caleb Coaty, of Klamath Falls, joined us for the afternoon hunt. We dozed in our blinds. A tiny bird picked its way through the tules, finding its food in the safety of the reeds. We inspected each other from three feet away.

We were saying goodbye to waterfowl season and hello to spring. It was my second goose hunt of the season; for Roe, it was his 117th day in the marsh. Roe had positioned me at the point of the tules where I had the best view and the best shot.

Caleb Coaty with a late-season limit: one white-fronted goose, a snow goose and two Ross geese.

"Four birds coming," I whispered. "Specks." We lowered our heads into the tules and watched between the reeds. They swung wide and then circled, lower now, at the extreme limit of the 20-gauge's range. Four specks circled again, but one seemed to distrust our setup and broke away. The other three tipped in and spread their wings.

My gun came up, stock welded to cheek, bead on its mark. Caleb's gun spoke second and Darren dropped the third bird as it turned. One skeptical speck sailed away toward the refuge with all the encouragement he needed.

DUCKS

Wing-Shooting and Waterfowl Habitat

Ducks and geese drifted in and out of my dreams. It's always hard to sleep the night before a hunt. When the alarm rang, I rolled out of bed and found my camo and my boots. An hour later, we tromped through icy marsh. A biting wind howled out of the west, driving a sullen sky.

Sage, Bill Herrick's Labrador, padded on top of the crust, while we broke through at every other step. We had to struggle through ice and wade to our waists to climb into the blind. With a head-high wall at the back and a low shelf in front, it was just what we needed to stay out of the storm, hidden from the birds.

"There!" A single teal went jinking over, with the wind that whistled in its wings. Bill scrambled for his still-unloaded shotgun and three more ducks – mallards – went by 30 feet off the deck in easy reach. If only we'd been ready for them. Sage stood, shivering from her swim to the blind.

A single drifted toward us, high on the wind. Bill shouldered his gun. "It's a little far, but I'm going to try," he said as he swung the barrel up. His finger tightened on the trigger and the greenhead folded to crash to the earth behind us.

Sage quivered with anticipation. "Fetch it up, Sage," Bill said, and the dog splashed down into the icy water and scrambled out onto dry ground.

While the dog and his master fetched the drake, two more mallards streaked by and I swung, led the second bird and missed. Twice. For the next two hours, we watched widgeon, teal, mallards and Canada geese drift by out of range.

Bill's hunting club owns a piece of property with several small lakes, east

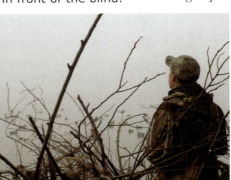

When setting up a spread of decoys, leave a spot for incoming birds to land, about 20 yards in front of the blind.

Residential
Commercial
All Utilities
Land Clearing
Digouts
Trucking
Septic

Justin Latham Excavation, Inc.
"Central Oregon's 2nd Generation Contractor"

(541) 480-6782   CCB# 177077
Serving All of Oregon

Custom Hunting and Fishing Plots
Food Plot Design and Installation
Inground Blinds
Water Features

of Bend. It is 23 acres of tall grass, tules and wetlands – a high desert habitat that supports cottontails, herons, marsh hawks, mergansers, cormorants, raccoons and other critters.

"It's all here for the wildlife, I come out and clear knapweed and do little projects to make this a good place for waterfowl and other animals. For four months out of the year – once a week or so – I hunt ducks," he said. "The birders come out from Bend and set up their binoculars and watch from over there," he said, pointing south. "We could develop it, but then this would all be gone."

People love nature in different ways. There are conservationist hunters, there are wildlife watchers and near-religious preservationists. To some, science-based management is irrelevant. But we knew hunters' efforts protect the land and animals, locally and around the world.

The people that make the difference are the hunters. Money raised from license fees, state waterfowl stamps and Federal duck stamps support science-based management and habitat enhancement. Banded together by conservation organizations like Ducks Unlimited and Oregon Hunters Association, the political force can work together for the good of wildlife.

WATERFOWL WEST OF THE CASCADES

Birds in the Pacific Flyway migrate from as far north as the Aleutian Islands all the way to the California coast. The Olympic Mountains and coastal areas of the outer Puget Sound support dense populations of harlequin ducks. The Copper River Delta produces the world's largest populations of trumpeter swans and dusky Canada geese. Upwards of

Bill Herrick tolls in a flock of widgeon while Sage looks on. The hunters had to break through ice and wade waist-deep to make it to the blind.

Resources for Hunters

Oregon River Maps & Fishing Guide (www.amatobooks.com)

ODFW WEBSITE: WWW.DFW.STATE.OR.US

DUCKS UNLIMITED: WWW.DUCKS.ORG

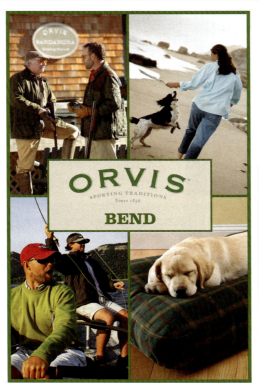

Visit our Bend retail store and discover the Orvis Distinctive Country Lifestyle.

The Orvis Bend team invites you to browse an extensive range of exclusive Orvis men's and women's apparel, world-renowned fly-fishing rods, reels, and tackle, hunting and shooting gear, unique gifts, and pet accessories.

Orvis Bend is located in the Old Mill District alongside the scenic Deschutes River.

Heading North: From the Parkway, take Colorado Avenue (Exit 138)
Heading South: From the Parkway, take Reed Market Road (Exit 139)

ORVIS BEND
320 SW Powerhouse Drive | Bend, OR 97702
For details, call 541-312-8200 or visit orvis.com/bend

10 million waterfowl use the Copper, Yakutat, Stikine, Tsiu and Susitna river flats in the spring.

Any habitat loss or degradation within the Pacific Flyway has an effect on the total population. Some of the issues include urban expansion, contamination of the estuary environment and loss of aquatic beds.

Funded by hunter dollars, conservation organizations work in concert with private landowners, foundations and corporations to protect and preserve wetlands.

Habitat restoration projects in Puget Sound and northern California benefit hunters in Oregon by providing healthy environments for ducks and geese at both ends of the Flyway.

Calvin Halladay after a morning in the marsh.

DUCKS AND GEESE IN THE GREAT BASIN

Over on the dry side of the Cascades, productive wetlands areas are limited. A component of the Pacific Flyway, the Great Basin is a major stopover on spring and fall migrations and a production area for mallards, canvasback, gadwall, redheads and cinnamon teal.

Projects in the Great Basin seek to preserve water quality and quantity to prevent outbreaks of disease and ensure habitat for resident waterfowl and birds passing through.

East of the mountains, the focus is to improve the use of water supplies on public and private lands and increase the habitat values that support migration and reproduction. Biologists and engineers work to restore marsh functions to support habitat that waterfowl use throughout the year, all supported by hunter dollars.

Anytime a waterfowl hunter takes to the marsh, he or she is making a positive difference for wildlife and habitat.

Whether the hunter travels halfway around the world, jump-shoots mallards on a meandering Willamette Valley stream, or climbs into a blind overlooking an ice-encrusted pond east of the mountains – every morning brings a new chance to take part in the age-old thrill that haunts our dreams.

Before taking to the marshes for ducks and geese, a hunter needs to have a state waterfowl stamp, a federal waterfowl stamp and a license, validated with Oregon's Harvest Information Program.

FLOAT-HUNTING FOR DUCKS

When leaves turn to gold and Vee's of waterfowl are on the wing, it's time to take your shotgun and camouflage out of the closet. Waterfowl season is here and there's no better place to slow down and focus on the hunt than on a river. If you don't have a dog or the patience to watch decoys but still want to hunt, try float-hunting for ducks in a canoe or drift boat.

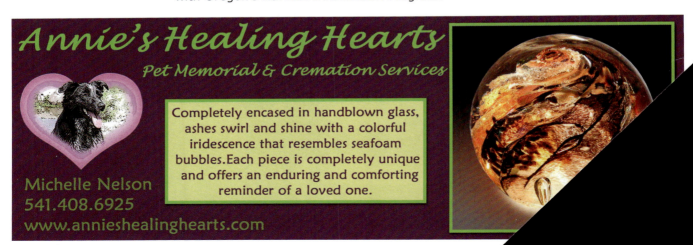

The tules provide natural cover as this hunter calls in the next flock.

Stream levels are down this year in many parts of the states so to float rivers like the Owyhee and the John Day, you may have to wait until after the first fall rains. In eastern Oregon, you can also drift for ducks in the Deschutes and on parts of the Crooked River.

West of the mountains, the Pudding, Clackamas, Willamette and Yamhill Rivers offer good hunting for waterfowl. Many lakes also provide great float-hunting opportunities.

It's not as simple as just finding a body of water with ducks on it. Jump-shooting requires the ability to move in close enough for a shot. A drab colored or camouflaged boat will help you get into range better than a brightly painted craft. Draw straws to determine the first shooter. Then trade places after an hour or so.

Select a body of water with plenty of cover for the birds to hide. Preferably one with back-eddies or small inlets, where the birds can rest away from wind and current. Move quietly and wait until they flush. Keep in mind, there may be other hunters on the water. (If those ducks you're watching aren't moving, it might be because they're decoys.)

To hunt ducks you need a State waterfowl stamp, an HIP (Oregon's Harvest Information Program) validation and a Federal duck stamp. If you plan to hunt close to a residential area, contact the nearest office of the ODFW to find out if there are any no-shooting zones that may apply.

In a canoe on a river, there's a sense of freedom at dawn, loading a shotgun while your breath turns to fog in icy air; life is at a slower pace, moving with the speed of the water.

Solitude waits around the next bend, or a sudden rush of wings against an autumn sky.

DOVES

For some hunters, opening day of dove season is the social event of the year. For others, it's a chance to pull shotguns out of the closet and tune up for fall hunts. Whatever reason you hunt doves, your best bet is to go early in the month.

Whether you shoot birds over maize near Madras, or on the stubble outside of Stayton, it's hard to deny the thrill of seeing dozens of doves, sweeping toward you and beyond with the sound of the wind in their wings

Doves like to roost in flocks, preferring denuded junipers adjacent to feed and water. In the morning they head out to feeding areas and typically will find shade for rest during the middle of the day. Feeding again in the late afternoon, they head to water, then to roosts in the evening.

They like to fly over water, so good stands can be taken along shallow streams or adjacent to farm ponds and cattle tanks. Set up stands at tree lines or where food is concentrated. In a valley, the birds will fly up and down the trough. A bare tree in the middle of a field is also a good location, especially if decoys are employed.

To a dove, good water is brackish and murky. In order for the birds to make it a regular watering hole, the bank must be bare or at least with little cover nearby to hide hungry predators. Scout for set-ups where a fencepost or a dead juniper will break up your outline. Once a hunter establishes the pattern of a particular group of birds, it is simply a matter of finding cover along the expected flight path.

Pick a spot with the sun at your back, beneath a tree, between barns, or behind a fence post. Someplace you can take advantage of concealment and still get good shots. Hunters that prefer pass-shooting might select an opening in the trees or a depression between two hills.

Doves are seedeaters, mostly ground-feeding on corn, wheat, sorghums and weed seeds. Look for doves on BLM lands near ranches, farms, and other easy feed sources. Watch open grasslands where grass and thistles have gone to seed. Walk the tree lines and look in the tops of dead snags where the birds like to rest. Look close to gravel roads in the evening when birds fill their crops.

The doves you hunt during the first week of the season are gone by the first hard rain or cold snap. But that gives you just enough time to clean your shotgun and buy a few more boxes of shells. Northern birds will drop in on the way south. Good dove hunting can be found through the end of the season.

North America's most common game bird, doves are found throughout the state, but some of the best hunting is in north central Oregon, from Redmond and Prineville, north to the Columbia and east to Ontario. Agricultural fields in the Willamette Valley and in the Umpqua Valley can yield good shooting and doves are common on the farms and ranches and BLM lands east of Klamath Falls.

A WINGSHOOTING CHALLENGE There is no bigger wingshooting challenge than what you will find on September's dove fields. These birds are plumb hard to hit. You need an edge if you hope to bag enough for dinner.

The best way to put birds in the game bag is to improve your shooting. Train to focus on one part of one bird. Key on a dove's beak for a passing shot or the tail feathers as it goes straight away. The tighter the focus, the better your chances are of bringing birds home for dinner.

While it is difficult to remember in the heat of the action, it is easily practiced on any bird you see. In time it becomes automatic.

There are more techniques to help the bird hunter fill the game bag. The first is timing. Take it slow. I find that when I let the excitement get the better of me, I shoot before the gun is mounted against my shoulder. I always miss when I rush the shot.

With an unloaded gun, practice disengaging the safety and shouldering it. The cheekpiece should come against your cheek, with the butt anchored against your shoulder. The barrel should be in the same plane as your master eye, front bead on (or ahead of) the target.

Picture the shot leaving the barrel in a string, similar to water in a hose. Imagine swinging a spray nozzle across the sky. When you swing your barrel, following through as you squeeze the trigger, your shot will 'wash' the target in the same way.

A stool can improve your shooting. Lunging from a crouched position to shoot is awkward. Rising easily from a chair promotes good stance and shooting position.

Camouflage clothing is ideal, but any drab outerwear will do. Many hunters use semi-automatic or pump shotguns. A variable or screw-in choke enables the hunter to vary the shot pattern, depending on the range of the birds. An improved cylinder or modified choke with No. 7-1/2 or 8 shot normally works best.

Another essential are earplugs. There may be more shooting on one dove hunt than in all the rest of your season's bird hunts combined. Earplugs keep you from flinching, but more important, they economize the auditory organs. You want to keep your hearing sharp so, on opening day of dove season 20 years from now, you can still hear the whistle of the wind in their wings.

ANIMAL EMERGENCY CENTER
Emergency & Critical Care for Small Animals
541-385-9110
www.bendaec.com

OPEN EVENINGS, WEEKENDS & HOLIDAYS
Hours :: Mon-Thurs 5pm to 8am
Fri 5pm thru Mon 8am

1245 SE 3rd St, Ste C3
Bend, OR

VALLEY QUAIL

A gust of wind blew a few yellowed leaves down the road and raindrops spattered on the front porch. I shrugged into my coat and wondered why summer had to leave without even whispering goodbye.

I was headed out the door when I heard the birds. Whit-WHIT-woo. Whit-WHIT-woo. They were in the yard and on the fence clucking nervously before taking to the air – a dozen valley quail – whirring away as Molly, my bird-hunting beagle, walked a little too close.

Whenever I see Molly and quail in the same vicinity, I think of the day we found a few of the top-knotted birds in the sage on the slope of a hill. It was a frosty morning and they led her off, flushing as she caught up to them. I managed three for three and picked up a single on the way back. I imagine that the scent of quail reminds her of the same day.

When the last of the birds buzzed away, I smiled. Molly's tail wagged and she had a little bounce in her step that seemed to say she is glad that summer is finally over and the real excitement is just around the corner.

The mountains and plains and river canyons of Oregon support 11 species of upland birds. By participation, valley quail rank fourth in the hearts of Oregon hunters, but in harvest they come a close second to chukar. Over ten years, an average of 11,000 hunters bag more than 90,000 birds.

CONNECT THE DOTS

Thanks to trap-and-transplants going on since the 1870s, quail can be found in almost every county, but the best hunting is east of the Cascades. Quail make their home in and around The Dalles, Hermiston, Pendleton, La Grande, Baker City, Ontario, Burns, Lakeview, Klamath Falls, Bend, Prineville and John Day. Draw a line between any of these towns and you are in quail country.

Best of all, 53% of Oregon is owned/managed by the Bureau of Land Management and the US Forest Service. Access is not hard to find.

If there's anything easy about quail, it is finding habitat. Where the four essential elements of habitat come

Finding Your Way

Much of eastern Oregon is owned by State and Federal agencies. Use a Bureau of Land Management map to help you determine the ownership of the land before you hunt. For the largest selection of maps east of the Cascades, including BLM maps, call Bend Mapping at 541-389-7440 or visit www.bendmapping.com.

Tim Curry
(541) 420-9393

CENTRAL OREGON SPORTING DOG
Dog Training | Breeding | Dogs For Sale

65030 Gerking Mkt. Rd. Bend, Oregon 97701
tim@oregonsportingdog.com

www.oregonsportingdog.com

> **Upland Access**
> The Oregon Department of Fish and Wildlife manages wildlife areas, most of which offer some type of upland game bird hunting opportunity. ODFW also works with private land-owners to encourage public access. Some of these private lands are enrolled in Regulated Hunt Areas (RHAs), Access and Habitat, and the Upland Cooperative Access Program. For hunting opportunities, click on the following web sites:
> www.dfw.state.or.us/resources/visitors/wildlife_areas_hatcheries.asp
> www.dfw.state.or.us/AH/hunting/
> www.dfw.state.or.us/resources/hunting/upland_bird/access/UCAP_brochure.pdf

A tiny patch of cover can hold a covey. Gary Lewis and his bird-hunting beagle bounced a bunch of birds to bag this male.

often pay off with a covey of quail.

Sunrise to mid-morning is the best time to watch for feeding birds. They are seldom far from cover. Sage, willow thickets, young aspen groves, leafy bushes or conifers will be close by. In our state, much of their range is on private land, though good hunting can be found on public ground as well.

In late afternoon, walk feeding areas near water. Listen for their calls, but pay close attention in the evening, as birds reassemble prior to roosting. When you spot a bevy, keep your dogs close, allowing them to search out the birds when you get into position.

In these days of pay-to-play access on private land and more hunters crowded into less acreage, together – water, food, space, and cover – the chances of locating birds increase substantially.

With a year-round water source at hand the chances of finding the birds increase. When water is abundant, birds may be dispersed and harder to find.

A long season gives hunters almost four full months of quail hunting in Oregon

River canyons are reliable reserves that support big coveys early in the season before fall rains bring water to the desert. A float down the John Day, the Deschutes, the Snake, the Owyhee or the Grande Ronde can pay off with multiple hunts up side canyons. The Crooked River, the Malheur, the Silvies, the Umatilla and the Imnaha rivers, while not as floatable, also hold a lot of quail (and chukar) within an easy walk of the waterline.

FIND THE BIRDS Food and cover are synonymous. Where blackberries and wild grapes grow, there may be a covey of quail close by. Quail are often found around old homesteads too, thriving on the crops that were once planted and now return voluntarily each year. While bird hunting, I never miss a chance to walk around an old pile of brush or broken down equipment. Such places

Often found along the edges of rangelands, quail utilize sagebrush for cover and feed. Invest the effort to hunt the far reaches of the area first. Many coveys go relatively untouched by hunters who don't have the heart to reach them.

it's hard to think of a more agreeable quarry than quail. National forests, wildlife areas and timber company acreage provide an abundance of ground and opportunity.

Oregon, with its high percentage of public land, offers the traveling wingshooter miles and miles of skyline and crooked canyons. Best of all, it's his own country owned in common with every other American. All you need is a map, a gun, a dog, a compass and good boots. The real excitement is just around the corner. ∎

MOUNTAIN QUAIL

Mountain quail sightings are short affairs punctuated by whirrs of wings and palpitations of the heart, but a hunter is more likely to hear mountain quail before he sees them. These birds seem to operate under the philosophy that a quail should be heard and not seen. An alarm call cle-cle-cle is the sound a hunter is most often to hear. After the covey is disturbed, mountain quail regroup with a series of whistled how-how-how assembly calls.

Mountain quail can be found east of the Cascades, but the best advice is to 'go west young quail hunter.'

This is the most overlooked bird hunt in the state, if not the continent. Most coveys go un-hunted over the course of a year.

The birds thrive on the brushy edges of conifer forests and streams. They eat the fruit of the blackberry, elderberry, hackberry, seviceberry, Oregon grape, gooseberry, poison oak and manzanita. Mountain quail make good use of pine nuts, clover, and the seeds of weeds and grasses. The quail roost under heavy brush or in small trees, and home territories can take in large areas. When winter comes, they head to lower elevations, following the snowline down.

The best concentrations of mountain quail can be found in the Coast Range and in the Cascades.

Because of the habitat, few upland game birds are as difficult. They run at the sight of a hunter. Drifts are likely to move ahead of the dog, but once they flush, in the rhododendrons and conifers, a pointing dog can find singles holding tight.

Mountain quail habitat, though daunting to the hunter, is not hard on the dog. The forest floor may be steep, but it is padded with leaf litter and the dark organic material left by moldering pine needles; Water is abundant.

Groups of quail generally number seven to nine birds. They do not form large coveys, but hunters sometimes see loose groups of birds feeding in the same area.

Typical quail habitat is between 2500 and 6000 feet above sea level, in the regrowth of an old logging area or burn and coveys may be widely scattered. Since they live on steep, brushy hillsides, a good way to hunt them is to ride logging roads on a mountain bike until the birds are spotted.

Stormy Weather Kennels and Royal Flush Hunting Preserve

Breeder of German Shorthair pointers and field-bred English Cockers

Gene Adams
541.410.2667

7878 SW Copley Rd
Powell Butte, OR 97753

CHUKAR

On the horizon, a dusting of snowcapped Iron Mountain to the north and the Ochocos to the south. Cumulus clouds drifted with a stiff wind against the clear blue sky.

Gary Madison, a pro dog trainer from Burns, Oregon, had Ace, an English pointer, and Bud, a German shorthair, on short leads. We were hunting the Himalayan chukar, high above the John Day River.

Gary had his black cowboy hat pulled down tight against the wind. He pointed. "We'll start on top of that first butte." Ace and Bud swung their noses into the breeze and strained against their tethers. The scent of chukar.

We crossed the top of the hogback and eased into a basin. A lone chukar broke out and away before we could get into position.

"That's Crazy Man Rock," Madison said, pointing at a boulder. "I brought a guy up here and he sat down right there. I asked him how he liked chukar hunting and he said, 'It is crazy, man. In fact, it's insane. I'm quitting right here.' So I left him on the rock," Madison said, "and hunted around that butte. When I got back, he was still sitting right there and I'd bagged six birds."

We swung around the crown of a hill. The wind wailed 20 miles per hour. We found the birds in a shallow depression between outcroppings. Ace locked up and I tried to walk in below, but I was still out of position when the birds erupted from the sage.

If there's one great 'everyman's hunt' left in these United States, where a hunter can walk his own (public) ground for miles, it's in pursuit of the Himalayan import called the chukar. A guide isn't necessary, but there's a lot to learn about how weather and hunting pressure influence the birds' habits.

Tiffany Lewis with a brace of chukar bagged on a December hunt.

ADVANTAGE EARLY

This transplant from Eurasia makes part of its living on another transplant from the same region: cheatgrass. Where you find the best cheat, you'll find birds. But cheatgrass is only part of a chukar's diet. In one study, 91 different foods were found in the crops of 87 chukar. Russian thistle, grasses, dandelions, wheat, fruits and seeds were well-represented.

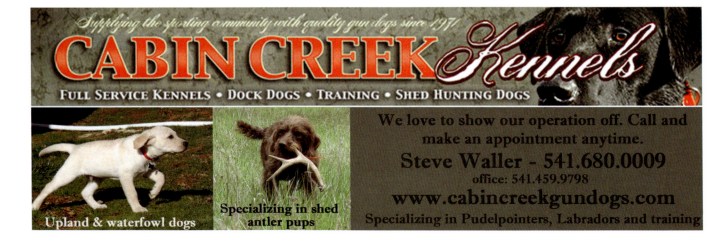

10% of the diet included insects. Though chukar thrive in and around sagebrush habitats, sage doesn't account for much of a chukar's diet.

Living is good early in the season. The birds do well in a dry environment, as long as there is water nearby. They are as predictable as it gets, feeding down the slope to water in the morning and again in the evening.

Look for tracks in dried mud near a waterhole and for fresh droppings. If the birds are eating grasses, the stools will appear green and white. A diet of seeds and roots manifest in a brown dropping.

In the summer and early fall, the birds frequently take dust baths, which create oval depressions in the loose soil.

Find the feed and follow the chow line. It might be in the green fringe along a creek or around a stock tank.

From the flats to the tops of the cliffs, you may find chukar anywhere, but certain types of habitat hold more birds. Look for features that seem out of place: where the green shows against a dry brown hillside, where a bump in the ground provides shelter from the wind, or a rocky outcropping on an otherwise bare hill.

Chukar start feeling the pressure on opening day, but their patterns don't change appreciably until after the first heavy rains in November.

AFTER THE RAINS With water on the desert, the birds are able to disperse into smaller coveys. When the water is easy to find in the hollow of a rock and on the stems of grass, chukar don't have to feed all the way down to the river.

Now, with moisture in the ground, tiny shoots of green grass push up through the soil. Brown hillsides take on a verdant hue. The green-up draws birds into smaller coveys and disperses them across a wider range. They feed on green grasses and broadleaf plants.

At this stage of the season, the hunter is likely to find smaller coveys. Birds will be spread across a larger area and may cover more ground as they prospect for new growth.

This is the time of year when you're most likely to find chukar on flat ground. Grassy mesas and hilltops may hold scattered coveys, at least until hunting pressure pushes them back down into the canyons.

It's the tension, three-toed tracks by the waterhole and a single hidden in the bunchgrass. It's the ache you feel in your muscles, a blur of wings and the thump of the gun.

Studies suggest that east-facing terrain holds the most promise. One researcher found almost 90 percent of chukar nests occurred on southeast slopes. And this aspect most often coincided with the best chukar feed.

Use the time between points to scout. Chukar droppings are about an inch in length. Older droppings appear tan in color, while the fresh stools appear green with a white uric acid cap. Find fresh droppings and you'll know at what elevation the birds are feeding.

By this time of the season, the younger birds have gained some experience. Now, at the first sign of danger, the covey begins to move. They'll run uphill and a few will disperse and hide. Anticipate at what point the birds might flush. If they're moving to the crest of a hill, they'll bust loose when they get there. If the dog goes on point, circle him and work back in from 40 yards out. Watch the dog's eyes for a clue as to where he last saw a bird.

After the flush and the shots, reload quickly and wait to see if the dog picks up another scent. There may be a single or two left in the grass.

Anticipate, Anticipate, Anticipate

The first thing a chukar hunter learns is that these birds run uphill and fly downhill. True enough, but chukar seek their food at a certain elevation for a reason. When they flush, chances are that after they swoop around that hill out of sight, they hit the ground to feed at the same elevation on the other side of the ridge.

By carefully studying a detailed map, you can figure out where they're headed. Use a topographic map and plan the hunt in advance.

Knowing the prevailing wind patterns is a big advantage. A dog needs the wind in his face before he can smell a bird. Don't put a handicap in the way, start the hunt where the wind is in your favor. Push the birds and go where they're going. At the end of it, your dogs will lock up for a last, spectacular flush.

Use a compass late in the season. Chukar seek out the south-facing slopes in cold weather. Don't waste time and energy looking for birds where they're not likely to be.

Chukar can be found in almost all the major river drainages in eastern Oregon. The more rugged and inhospitable the terrain, the better.

One of the best ways to locate birds is to listen. Take a break and tune in. If you busted the covey, they'll want to regroup and the only way they know to do that is to call, usually within 15 minutes after they've been disturbed. When the birds are calling, they are on the move and when they are on the move, they are headed uphill, toward cover

LATE IN THE GAME Late season chukar are toughest of all. They sneak, they run, and when they fly, they go like fighter jets, close to the ground, flat-out in a blur of wings and sound.

With cold wind, persistent rain, and ice and snow on the desert, the south-facing slopes are more likely to hold chukar. And the birds won't stay as close to their water source when the sky brings it to them.

On windy days, the birds seek out shelter, which might mean craggy rimrock, a draw choked with sagebrush, or even a rocky depression just off the crown of a hill. It doesn't take much cover to hide a 10-inch bird.

When the weather gets rough, chukar migrate down. In heavy snow, the birds find feed and cover in habitat more typically associated with quail, hiding in the willows down along the creek.

But when the snow lets up, look at the hilltops again. High wind can sweep the hilltops clear of snow and birds will find it. Chukar seek out remnant cheatgrass seeds and any green grasses that might appear, given a little sun and a thaw.

An English Setter on point. *Photo courtesy Bar Lee Setters*

This part of the season is characterized by running birds and long flushes. Even the young-of-the-year know enough to go on alert when they hear the slam of a car door, or humans shouting commands to dogs. An entire flock might freeze when alerted by the sentry. When danger approaches, they move off, running low to the ground. And they don't wait around for dogs to go on point and hunters to walk up and shoot them.

A tactic that often pays is to hunt down from above. When the dog goes on point, the bird wants to fly downhill. Get between the bird and its escape route. To get around you, the bird will have to tower, or flush sidehill. Both scenarios make for better shooting.

When freezing fog is a component of the hunt, birds are easier to approach. You just have to know where they are. Now is a great time to have some way to locate the dog on point. One of the new GPS-assisted collars can help you find the dog. A collar with an automatic hawk scream can also hold the birds and help the hunters get into position in front of the dog.

In fact, a lot of hunters miss out on this one. Hawks make their living on chukar, huns and quail. If you see the avian competition hunting in an area, there's a good chance you found the birds.

There was a hawk hunting ahead of us on that January day. We followed.

Ace pointed the covey on a finger ridge. Madison, silent, scribed a half-circle with his left index finger and I swung in, twenty yards in front of the pointer. Ace glanced at his owner and then back at the birds. I followed his gaze. Where were they?

A dozen in the air. Focus. Square up. Get down on the wood. Squeeze.

Ace found the bird and brought it to his master's feet. Bud pointed the next covey and I knocked another bird down.

I felt the right knee go first, a flare of pain as a rock twisted underfoot. An old fishing injury, haunting me in the highlands. And then the left ankle. And then the left knee.

Down in a canyon, we lost track of Ace. Madison climbed the hill, found the dog on point and killed a chukar. Before he came back down, I heard the report of his gun a second time.

That hawk was still hunting, two feet above the ground now. I knew I should follow Madison, but my knees wouldn't let me. I sat on a rock for a few minutes and rested. The truck was a silver speck a mile below. It was crazy, man.

HUNGARIAN PARTRIDGE

Huns have an understated beauty, with a form that follows function. Wings of white and mottled brown allow the bird to hide from predators by holding still. A pastel-grey on the breast blends on the head with shades of brown. Their eyes are surrounded by a pencil-thin border of red. Flanks and breasts are splotched with markings of chocolate brown.

Hungarian partridge are birds of the wide open spaces and can be found in cropland, sage, and bunchgrass country. Look for foothill habitat close to irrigated ag lands for the best hunting.

Hunters find the birds in short, light cover. Huns feed mainly on grains like corn, oats, wheat and barley, but also eat weed seeds and green leaves.

Huns begin feeding after most of the dew dries off the grass. They feed until late morning, loaf in a grassy area until mid-afternoon, then resume feeding until dusk. The birds roost in alfalfa fields, grain stubble, short grass or even on plowed ground. They often form roosting rings. In winter, huns may roost in a depression in the snow, or burrow-roost under it.

Coveys normally consist of 10 to 12 birds. Huns do not hold well when first approached. They tend to sneak ahead of a hunter or dog, then burst from cover in unison. The covey remains together. Early in the season, huns fly only a short distance. As the season progresses, they go farther, sometimes over half a mile.

Shotguns and shells used for huns are similar to those used for chukars. Some hunters prefer 12-gauge guns with full chokes in late season.

Huns are as spooky as chukar, faster than quail, and smart enough to run, circle and hide. Add to all that its taste on the table and this import from Hungary is a welcome and worthy quarry for the best dogs and hunters.

Hunters may encounter huns while in the field for chukar. Huns are birds of the wide open spaces and can be found in cropland, sage and bunchgrass country from Madras north to the Columbia, east to the Snake River and south to the Steens. Generally, rolling foothill habitat close to irrigated agricultural lands provides the best action for Hungarian partridge.

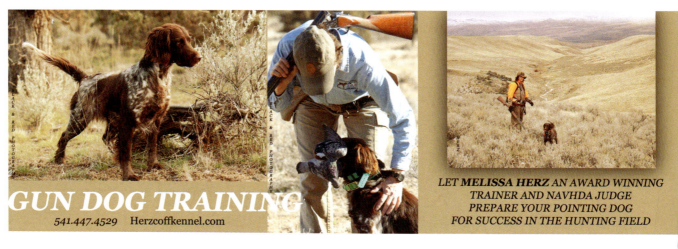

LET MELISSA HERZ AN AWARD WINNING TRAINER AND NAVHDA JUDGE PREPARE YOUR POINTING DOG FOR SUCCESS IN THE HUNTING FIELD

GUN DOG TRAINING
541.447.4529   Herzcoffkennel.com

FOREST GROUSE

I don't know how it is where other people hunt grouse, but the best I hope for is a chance.

The grouse were there last year when the elk were not. I carried a rifle instead of a shotgun, but I marked the spot in my memory and last month found my way there again.

Left of the trail there was a marsh, right of the trail, rhododendrons and firs. Grouse were in the path. One was in the open, a whirr of wingbeats from the wall of cover.

My chance. I took it, the bird in motion, the 20-gauge swinging with it. Smoke still curling from the barrel, I broke the gun, thumbed the empty out and pushed another shell in.

There were more birds, but they were in the rhododendron now, ruffed brown blurs that vanished like vapor.

With three hours before dark and two birds left in my three-bird limit, there might be another chance. But I doubted it.

Grouse was the first game I brought to the table many years ago and to my taste, it has no equal. It would probably keep well in the freezer, but I never let it wait that long. This time we sautéed it with spinach, tomatoes, onions and mushrooms in melted butter.

There is no mistaking the flush of a grouse. Like a jet plane, they blast from the cover, sometimes almost beneath your feet. Thus imprinted on the brain, the hunter learns fast which ground is

Grouse are commonly found in brushy areas adjacent to swampy lowlands and on the steep hillsides above. Birds often feed on high benches that offer a quick downhill escape.

likely to hold the birds.

Ruffeds inhabit brushy areas of mixed hardwoods, adjacent to swampy lowlands or steep hillsides, along the edges of clearcuts, creeks, swamps, meadows, and where thick growth meets a stand of timber. Many times, birds can be found on high benches that offer a quick escape downhill.

Because grouse feed on insects, you can find them on the edge of fields where alder or aspen groves provide cover. Ruffed grouse also feed on berries or ripened fruit around old orchards and homesteads.

Blue grouse are hunted in coniferous forests at higher elevations than ruffed grouse. Walk the ends of open ridges early and late in the day, midday, watch the trees for resting birds.

Blues can be flushed along the edges of meadows near thick timber or on the slopes of more open, timbered areas. They eat berries, green leaves, flowers, seeds and insects in the summer and fall. With the absence of these in the winter, they turn to the needles of the conifer trees.

Confine your scouting to areas close to water and hunt blue grouse by searching along timbered hilltops and the brush just outside a stand of timber. During the middle of the day they sometimes rest in the trees and can be spotted in the treetops.

Forest grouse can be found throughout the state. Old burns are a good place to start. Hunters can find good grouse hunting where new growth pushes up through the ashes.

One summer, a friend and I hiked in to a spot in the Ochocos where a B-18, en route to Alaska from an air base in California, was lost with all hands on board. The four crewmen were on a winter wartime mission in 1942. Flying low over the mountains, the plane clipped the tops of tall pines and crashed on the edge of what is now the Black Canyon Wilderness.

Wild fires have erased what remains there might have been. Almost 70 years later there is little left to mark the site save the broken trees and an opening in the canopy. I circled the site on blown-down timber and found where deer had fed on the new growth in the wake of last year's blaze.

One foot in front of the other, I walked a fallen tree up the hill. Ahead of me, a blue grouse blasted into flight. I'd left my shotgun at home, but the spot is marked in my memory. I'll get another chance.

Ruffed grouse and blue grouse are some of the most available but under-hunted upland birds in our state. Public land birds are available to anyone with a full tank of gas and a shotgun.

Other species are quicker to run or flush, but a grouse holds tight while a hunter walks by. Its plumage blends so perfectly you may never see the bird until it breaks away in a blur of wings and sound. The best you can hope for is a chance.

From the Columbia south to the California border, look for ruffed and blue grouse among the firs and pines of western Oregon and down the eastern reaches of the Cascades. In southern Oregon, there are grouse in the Klamath Basin and east to Lakeview. In eastern Oregon, there are grouse to be found in the Ochocos, Elkhorns and the Blue Mountains. ■

541.419.5809
Ross Harris

744 NW Dogwood Ave
Redmond, OR 97756
Ross_Harris8@hotmail.com
Licensed, Bonded & Insured
CCB# 144501

Wolf Custom Painting

SAGE GROUSE

Short Sage Grouse Season Offers Hunters a Different Bird Hunting Experience

The dirt road took us about 30 miles from the highway around a mountain, through a large basin and up to a long, treeless plateau. A long, billowing cloud of dust marked our progress through the desert.

We found the water, a lake that had shrunk over the summer to become little more than a mud puddle. A one room cabin stood guard over this waterhole and we parked close by, and looked through its windows at a building now claimed by packrats.

A dry bed, once planted in grain, surrounded the little lake and cabin. A seemingly endless sea of sage stretched in all directions.

This was a very important mud puddle, we found out as we walked its perimeter. Cattle, antelope, rabbit, coyote and sage grouse sign were there in the soft mud that surrounded the water.

We were here to hunt sage grouse, having drawn controlled hunt tags for this unit. It was the middle of the afternoon and our only day to

Sage grouse are the largest birds in the grouse family. Their plumage is mottled gray in appearance and the birds blend perfectly with the sagebrush.

hunt these birds in a five-day season. We had been traveling all day, hunting for water mainly. Now that we had reached our destination we could either take a nap in the sun and wait for the birds to come to us or we could go after them, hoping to flush them from the sage. It was an easy decision. It was time to go hunting.

Rich walked east and I headed into the sun. Hunting without dogs this time, we had to concentrate on the likeliest cover, zigging and zagging to flush grouse. There were small birds flying ahead of me, low over the tops of the sage. I turned to see how Rich was doing and watched him suddenly swing his gun into the air, sunlight glinting from the barrels of the shotgun.

A grouse was in the air and I heard the sound of his gun. A single shot and the bird was down. From a distance I watched while he retrieved it and lifted it above his head to show me. He put the bird in his game bag and continued east while I headed west.

His gun spoke again after a few minutes. Two distant thumps as two more birds lifted into the air and made good their escape.

We joined forces again after awhile. Rich cleaned his bird, a young female, while I watched and took pictures. We hunted into the evening together, walking twenty to thirty yards apart. Where the sage met a corner of the dry lake bed, Rich surprised another pair. One fell to his gun, his bag limit now filled, while the other bird flushed across in front of me. I missed the big grouse with both barrels and watched it fly out across the sage.

Now it was back to the truck as the sun sank lower in the west. Rich cleaned his second sage grouse, this one a big male. He kept a wing from each of his birds to send to the Department of Fish and Wildlife.

Since 1982, sage grouse hunters have turned in wings taken each season. Hunters have provided more than 5,000 wings from birds and these wings are evaluated at what biologists call 'wing bees' where the information each wing offers is read by one of several biologists.

PINE COUNTRY OUTFITTERS
- CLOTHING & ACCESSORIES
- QUALITY FIREARMS SALES
- WORLDWIDE HUNTING & FISHING TRIPS
- CUSTOM FLY RODS

BERETTA
CZ-USA

PHONE 541-706-9295

1441 SW CHANDLER AVE STE 101 - BEND, OR 97702

Biologists glean information about the overall health of the sage grouse population, as well as ratios of male to females and juvenile birds to older birds. Successful nesting can also be determined from the wings of adult females. This is added to the information gathered at the strutting ground surveys. This helps guide the department's management of the species.

With Rich's birds in the bag it was now time to find a bird for me to take home. Rich helped me work the cover we had searched earlier as the sun sank to the horizon. In the last minutes of shooting light we watched the water hole but no birds came in. As I unloaded my gun at the truck I saw an owl that had come to hunt, swooping low over the sage, pursuing his prey along the ground. You know, rubbing it in.

The sage grouse hunt for most bird hunters requires extra effort for little return in meat, but the experience makes up for it. Desert hunters may see, as we did, antelope, wild horses, coyotes and rabbits.

Every year, eastern Oregon offers a hunt for sage grouse on the dry side of the Cascades. It is a controlled hunt and a bird hunter must apply for the privilege.

In the 1800s, up to 1.1 million sage grouse could be found in parts of what are now 16 western states and three provinces. In 1998, the rangewide estimate was that the springtime sage grouse population numbered 157,000. Habitat disruption and destruction probably accounted for most of the decline.

A mottled-brown bird, with black and white camouflage, the mature male sage grouse can weigh up to seven pounds and stretch the tape to 30 inches from his beak to the tip of his tail.

To find sage grouse, locate the water and large three-toed tracks in the mud around the edges. The birds return to water at evening and can be hunted in the sage nearby. Most hunters use No. 4 lead shot.

Sage grouse habitat in eastern Oregon. Because the birds need water and this is mainly a desert hunt, the grouse are often found close to water sources.

Sage grouse need habitat that is made up of 70% sagebrush and 30% grasslands. That type of ground covers roughly 25% of the state, extending east and south from the city of Bend. For nesting, sage grouse seem to prefer taller cover, while low sage flats are better for leks, winter habitat and early brood rearing.

Seasons are set in August each year. Sage grouse season takes place in mid-September and lasts between five and eight days. For season dates, visit the Oregon Department of Fish and Wildlife web site (www.dfw.state.or.us). The season bag limit is two sage grouse.

The Whitehorse, Beatys Butte, Warner, Beulah and Malheur River units are the most popular hunts. Eastern Oregon roads are rough and services are few and far between. Bring a high-clearance four-wheel drive and make sure to check the air in the spare.

Much of eastern Oregon is owned by State and Federal agencies. Use a Bureau of Land Management map to help you determine the ownership of the land before you hunt.

www.LAKEINTHEDUNES.com

- Trophy Trout Fly-Fishing
- Sporting Clays Course
- Upland Bird Hunts
- Varmint Hunts
- Waterfowl

All trips are booked individually **Russell Scott - 541.633.3120**

PHEASANT

PHEASANT TACTICS: FIVE RUSES FOR MORE ROOSTERS

Dried rows of corn rattled with the November breeze. The old side-by-side rode light in my right hand. I ducked to get a glimpse through the uncut stalks and spied a skulking rooster.

We had boxed the corner of the standing corn. The drivers busted up through the ten-foot stalks. They whistled, howled like coyotes and shouted. There were pheasants and quail feeding on the corn and as the drivers approached, they ran skittering away toward our corner, to circle on the ground or take to the air.

Following the drivers' progress, I was startled to hear a sudden rush of wings behind me as a rooster leapt skyward. Turning, I shot too soon, then took a better shot.

We pushed fields of standing corn, fallow hillsides, fence lines stacked with tumbleweeds and soggy bottomland. Pheasants would burst from cover hundreds of yards away to soar onto the next property or hold to flush with a roar of wings almost at the toes of our boots. Drives were structured to give everybody a chance. Responsibility and muzzle control were constantly stressed above the bagging of game.

When necessary, we walked in a straight line, six abreast across a field. One hunter shouldn't lag behind the rest, nor should another get too far ahead. That ordered hunt for wild birds taught me about roosters and the strategy it takes to put them in the game bag.

Paxton Eicher admires a cagey rooster he bagged at the end of a soggy central Oregon hunt.

The hunt is a magic act – the hunter is the magician and the pheasant the jaded audience that has seen it all before. Whatever trick you decide to pull out of the bag depends on the habitat and the number of stage hands (hunting partners) you have at your disposal. As any good magician knows, you have to understand your crowd.

Pheasants love 'edge,' that fringe habitat found at the borders of cropland and scrub, the stream banks and ditches that border fields of grain. In the morning, they prefer sunlight to shade.

If a rooster has survived a season or two, don't expect him to spend much time with the hens. If the ladies are headed one way, you can bet a long-tailed rooster is

---

PHEASANT AND CHUKAR HUNTING
August 1 - March 31

- Perfect place to start new hunters
- Self-guided or guided hunts
- Clay shooting and instructions
- Overnight accommodations and RV parking available
- Reward-based dog training, boarding and conditioning year round

Olex preserve

Arlington, Oregon   Phone: 541-454-2011   www.olexbirdhunting.com

headed the other.

The rooster has one goal in the fall, his survival. He's been on the menu everyday of his life, outwitting foxes, coyotes, bobcats, owls and hawks. When autumn comes, you're just another predator with opposing thumbs and a shotgun. He'll beat you too, unless you change it up with a few tactics he hasn't encountered.

Pheasants roost in medium height grass and awake before sunrise to pick grit and gravel. Next, they head to the fields to feed in the first glow of the new day. By shooting hours, they are working back out of the grain into the fringe cover. Mid-morning, with the sun already high in the sky, will find the birds in the thickest, densest cover they can find, lying low until late afternoon.

At the close of the day, with the birds on the move, is the best time since morning to spot and flush them along the fringes of feeding cover.

After opening weekend, birds have learned that the slam of a car door and the whump of a shotgun signal the approach of hunters. While we are mapping out our action, the pheasants are planning to exit stage left. Remember, you're playing in their theater and they know the acts better than you do.

The first rule is to pick your ploy. You need drivers and blockers if you're going to put on the Grand Illusion. If there are only two of you, perform your sleight-of-hand in the fringe cover and leave the food plots to larger groups.

The second rule is to play the wind. Working into the wind, your pointer or flusher will smell the birds before he stumbles onto them. You'll be able to watch the dog's attitude and know when you're getting close.

To beat a pheasant at his own tricks, you need to call the strategy before you take to the field. Here are five ruses to help you bag more roosters.

1. THE SQUEEZE SUBTERFUGE.

This tactic is best when you've got six or more players. Come in quiet. Stop the car about a mile before the hunting field and let your dogs run off their early-morning excitement. You want to see that they're obeying commands and working close before they take the stage. Sketch the field and your hunt in advance. Drivers and blockers should have the plan in hand and know their positions. Turn off the music, don't slam the door and keep conversation to a whisper.

Give the blockers 15 minutes to get into position on the sides, as well as the ends, to take the advantage over birds that squeeze out the middle. Drivers can come in loud or quiet, depending on the game plan, but the best rule when working toward blockers is to keep the safety on until there is blue sky beneath the bird.

In a big field, a pheasant will run as far as it can before it takes to the air. At the edge, where the crops or the grass give way to a stream, a ditch, a road, or a stand of trees, expect the birds to flush wild.

2. THE ZIGZAG FEINT.

Employ this trick when there are fewer hunters and lots of good habitat. A measured, methodical, silent approach is the key. Stay ten yards apart, working from one edge to the other, in a zigzag fashion. Don't be in a hurry. When working brushy fence rows or ditches, one or two drivers should bust through the weeds with a dog, searching a slow zigzag pattern. Post another hunter at the end of the row to jump lurking birds into the air. Keep communication to a minimum so the moves aren't telegraphed to the birds.

Most hunters work a field by walking through, ten yards apart with the dog moving back and forth. The zigzag works the field in a thorough manner and keeps a rooster guessing.

When a bird is on the run, keep him between you and your partners. He's got you both located and as the noose tightens, he'll flush or hold.

When the dog goes on point, make a half-circle 20 yards out to come in looking straight at him.

Pheasants like edge habitat best of all. When the group is small, you can score by hunting smaller pockets and keeping a blocker at the end of the row.

Watch the dog's eyes. He knows where the bird is.

If possible, make your approach from below. When the bird flushes, it'll want to go downhill, unless you're blocking the exit. If it has to fly uphill, it has a lot of altitude to gain and you've got more time to take the shot.

When a bird escapes, watch its flight plan. It may hit the ground and start running or it might lock up and hide right where it landed. Mark and follow the flush after the first ruse has run its course.

🚩 3. THE SIDELINE STRATAGEM.

Pheasants live along the fringe. Moving from roost, to gravel, to feed and water are easiest in edge habitat. The lone hunter and a dog will make the most points on midday jaunts through fringe cover. Here the birds go to rest when the sun is high or to escape from the pressure a large group may be putting on a nearby crop field.

When hunting the edge of a river or lake, you may flush pheasants that have sought refuge on the fringes of nearby fields. They almost always fly over the water instead of back over the resting cover.

These birds have learned that at the first hint of danger, safety lies on the other side of the river. One property we hunt has ranches on both sides of the river, with an island in the middle. When there are parties hunting both banks, this is the only time these birds are in any real danger. The island is the last place of refuge. Except when I bring my waders.

This mindset also pays along railroad tracks. Where the cinders end and the bushes start is good escape cover. And the bird will most often fly across or along a railroad track, rather than breaking back into the fields.

Ditches are another sideline play. When pushed, a seasoned rooster knows how to use a ditch. Whether it is a dry irrigation canal or a barrow pit, he will use it to his best advantage. Once he hits the furrow, he'll go one way or the other at top speed.

🚩 4. THE TRIANGLE DECEPTION

Use this move when hunting long ditches or strip habitat, such as along a railroad track or a river. One hunter is the point of the triangle, moving through the cover about 50 yards ahead of the rest of the group. The other two hunters should take the edges, pushing a wedge into the pheasant habitat. As the birds in the deep cover move out to the edges, they'll be kicked up by the

Hunting Pheasants on Preserves

Imported to Oregon from Asia in the 1880s, the ringneck pheasant fast became an American favorite. The bird is a walking, flying kaleidoscope of color. Flashing blue, purple, copper and iridescent green, it rises out of the amber grain in a blur of wings and sound.

In the late 19th century, the state of Oregon was the hub of western pheasant hunting, but as farming practices changed and the birds took hold in other locales, the hotspots changed.

Today, many hunters have turned to preserves, where private land is managed for upland habitat and wild populations are supplemented with pen-reared birds.

A few companies offer lodging and meals. Some provide packages tailored to business groups, for hunts that may last three hours or three days. Almost all can provide a guide and a dog if you don't bring your own.

Preserve hunting for upland birds extends the season. On a licensed preserve, hunters may pursue gamebirds from August 1 through March 31.

Tall grass is hard to hunt because the birds could be anywhere. It pays to keep the bird between the hunters and let the dog work it out

BAR-LEE SETTERS

Central Oregon's Premier Gun Dog Trainer and Breeder of High Class English Setters

DOGTRA PRO FIELD STAFF
LARRY LEE
PO Box 8456
BEND, OR 97708
541 / 419 / 8228 CELL
541 / 382 / 7670 OFFICE

Bar-Lee's Miss Setting Sun

All training done with Positive Reinforcement and Repetition!

Bar-Lee's Casanova

**References available
Pups available seasonally
Pedigrees on request**

GUNDOGBREEDERS.COM/BREEDERS-OREGON/BAR-LEE-SETTERS.HTML

hunters at the base of the triangle.

The pheasant doesn't want to leave his hideout, so rather than flush, it would rather hold or sneak. Just when it gets around the point man, headed in the opposite direction, it runs into the next hunter.

5. THE FREEZE-OUT PLOY.

Pheasants expect a motion offense, but they don't know how it's coming. If the dogs get 'birdy,' but they don't find, lock up or flush, stop and try a freeze-out. What the roosters don't expect is for you to stop.

It doesn't take a lot of cover to hide a pheasant. I've flushed roosters from cover that wouldn't have hidden a mouse. These birds are the ones that count on stillness instead of foot speed. You can beat them at this game. Simply stop and call the dogs back for another pass. And then another. Hold your ground and wait the bird out. Either the dogs will find him, or he'll get nervous and make a break.

Even the hunter without a dog can make a pheasant crazy with the freeze-out. Start and stop at intervals, especially in the corners of fields, where the edge gives way to another type of habitat. Pheasants get nervous when a slow-walking hunter stops and waits. Even a tight-holding bird will get nervous and flush when it can't take the pressure.

Pheasants were brought from China and released in Linn County in 1882. Oregon's first pheasant hunt was held in 1891.

SAFE SHOOTING
Preserve hunting can offer a lot of shooting. Practice safe gun handling by observing shooting lanes and never shoot over another hunter's head. Wear hunter orange and don't shoot birds until they are in the air with blue sky beneath them.

THE FUNDAMENTALS OF DECEPTION

Plan your hunt and hunt your plan. Strategy comes first.

Don't foretell the effect. Go in quiet. Hunt with your face into the wind and slow down. Use blockers when you can and work the edges.

Avoid unnecessary actions. Keep the dogs in check with electronics or with leads until they get 'birdy.' Shouted commands and foot races to catch the dog will only put birds on alert.

Never repeat an effect. If you know there are birds left in the field you just hunted, let them filter back in and hit them the next day with a trick they haven't seen before. A good magician keeps his methods secret. Let other hunters make all the noise and run the birds to cover.

And let them wonder why you always bring home a limit.

Win or lose, the pheasant hunt is most glorious for what returns in memories. Good friends, hard-working dogs, long-tailed birds and sunlight on steel barrels. And a ruse that worked.

Some wise old birds head to the sagebrush when they hear hunters take to the field.

WILD TURKEY

Indians across the country ate a lot of turkey and used their feathers for decoration, but the Native Americans that made their home in the land we call Oregon, seldom saw a turkey feather. Here, a quill from Meleagris gallopavo *was a symbol of adventure. To get one, a hunter had to travel many sleeps to the east.*

Today, thanks to the foresight of the National Wild Turkey Federation and Oregon sportsmen, we have a turkey hunting tradition. And you don't have to travel far to find them.

Two young gobblers and four hens fed on the far side of the clearing on a bench among the oak trees. One of the jakes strutted while the others fed. I watched through my Alpen binocular and mentally measured spurs and beard. Characteristic of a jake, seven center feathers stood taller than the rest of his fan. He dragged his wingtips on the ground and displayed, back and forth.

I dragged my striker against the slate. The jake continued to strut. I changed the tone – putt, putt, putt – and the bird gobbled. I had his number, but my call brought in another young gobbler and his hens. He headed straight for me and my hen decoy and turned at five yards.

That's when it occurred to me it might be a difficult task to call gobblers where all the males already had hens. When even jakes have a flock, there are a lot of hens. Usually, the gobbler stays with the hens he knows rather than chasing the siren's call.

After twenty minutes had passed, I had nine gobblers and eleven hens at the far end of the clearing. One of the hens sported a four-inch beard. Half a dozen of the toms had beards so long they almost stepped on them. The jakes, now outclassed, gave ground. A grumpy old gobbler with a beat-up fan, kept the younger birds away.

I could afford to be picky. I wanted a long-spurred bird with an eight-inch beard.

After an hour, the birds began to separate. Two jakes with five hens headed my way. I putt-putt-putted on the call.

Bolder now, the dominant jake with a three-inch beard,

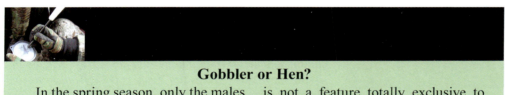

Gobbler or Hen?

In the spring season, only the males (called toms or gobblers) may be taken. First time turkey hunters may wonder if they could tell a male from a female. There are definite differences.

The crown of a gobbler's head is white, while its face is mainly blue and red. Male turkeys have a prominent snood, the mostly useless appendage that grows above the beak. A gobbler's noggin is completely bald while a female will have small feathers on her neck and head.

On the gobbler's breast there is a beard, a series of coarse hair-like fibers. On a jake (immature gobbler) it may be only three inches long. A mature male will have a beard approaching eight inches in length and longer. This is not a feature totally exclusive to gobblers though, as some females may sport a beard.

Another feature that sets toms apart is their spurs. Spurs are found on a gobbler's lower legs and will average between one half inch to an inch and a half long.

Maybe the best way to differentiate between the sexes is by looking at the coloration of the body. The tips of a hen's breast feathers are buff giving females a brownish look while a tom's breast feathers are tipped with black giving him an iridescent, polished sheen.

The Northwest Turkey Federation in Oregon

The NWTF is a 450,000-member grassroots, nonprofit organization with members in 50 states, Canada, and 11 foreign countries. It supports scientific wildlife management on public, private, and corporate lands, along with wild turkey hunting as a traditional North American sport.

The first Oregon chapters were formed in 1990. There are now 20 Oregon chapters, working to enhance game habitat and turkey hunting opportunities in western and eastern Oregon. NWTF pays for half the trap-and-transfer operations in partnership with the Oregon Department of Fish and Wildlife. The NWTF and ODFW have raised and spent almost $1 Million on projects within the state. Recent projects include establishment and maintenance of 4,950 acres of wildlife openings and habitat in the Ochoco National Forest, Wallowa-Whitman National Forest and on public-access private timberlands.

The NWTF also conducts Women in the Outdoors, Wheelin' Sportsmen (for men and women with disabilities), and Jakes (youth) outreach programs.

He couldn't get any satisfaction, so he headed up the hill with his hens.

In the afternoon, I set an ambush on a ridge top.

Puffed up, his tail in full fan, the boss bird's wattle was bright red, the skin around his eyes was blue and the top of his head was white as a Bald eagle's.

The longbeards strutted among the hens, strung out in a line inside the trees. A fence and the oak trees made them feel secure, but when the birds separated, I picked one of the toms and set the bead at the top of his head.

This bird had inch-long spurs, a beard that measured 8.25 inches and enough bulk to tip the scales to 18 pounds, the biggest turkey I've ever put on the table.

Wild turkeys can be found in every Oregon county. In the best turkey habitat, hunters spend between two and five days in the pursuit of their gobbler and average one bird for every three hunters.

A hunter can make use of nearly all the bird. Spurs can go on a necklace and the wing bone can be turned into a call like the Indians used. The beard can be kept as a trophy and the feathers turned into fly-tying materials or spun in a wreath for Thanksgiving. You'll need 60 tail feathers to complete a wreath. That means you'll need to bag at least three birds. Fortunately, we have a lot of turkeys in our state and the feather is still a symbol of adventure, of good days spent afield, a bow and arrow or a shotgun in hand.

OREGON'S BEST TURKEY HUNTING

Jackson County is one of the top turkey producing areas in Oregon. Highways 66 and 140 will take you to some good hunting country to the east, in a mixture of public and private land. Explore BLM land on backroads to the southwest of Talent and Phoenix.

The spring turkey hunt is a great way to introduce kids to the excitement of the hunt.

Highway 62, from Shady Cove to Prospect takes you through good habitat.

In Josephine County, turkeys can be found in the Rogue and Chetco valleys.

Almost all of Douglas County is turkey country. Most of the larger timber companies allow hunter access.

There are several good areas to hunt spring gobblers in Lane County. Explore the country from Eugene to Mapleton and south to Cottage Grove. East of I-5, there is good hunting from Dorena Reservoir to Oakridge, and Hills Creek Reservoir in the Willamette National Forest.

Benton County flocks are on the increase. Best opportunities can be found in the Alsea watershed and west of Corvallis.

Linn County hotspots include the area south of Sweet Home and Foster, and northwest to Lebanon. Look for Polk County turkeys near Rickreall and west of Monmouth. In Yamhill County, you can find turkeys northwest of McMinnville.

Washington, Tillamook, Columbia, and Clatsop Counties have some turkeys in the river valleys east of the Coast Range.

EASTERN OREGON In Klamath County, birds can be found east and west of Highway 97, but the best bet is to scout the Keno area, walking back-country roads and trails, looking for sign.

Lake County is often overlooked, but there are turkeys to be harvested. Try northeast of Lakeview and northwest along Highway 31, in the Fremont National Forest.

Central Oregon's best bets are in Crook County. Turkeys inhabit much of the Ochoco Mountains in the Ochoco National Forest. The best location is northeast of Prineville. Concentrate on the areas surrounding the Mill Creek and Bridge Creek Wilderness areas. The Maury Mountains also have turkeys and there are flocks surprisingly close to Ochoco and Prineville Reservoirs. To the east, turkeys can be found near Paulina and north to Rager Ranger Station.

Jefferson County's turkey hunting hotspot is Green Ridge, near Black Butte.

Consider Wasco County. The White River area is famous for its turkey hunting. Prospect for turkeys near Rock Creek Reservoir, Tygh Valley, Friend, Dufur, and The Dalles.

Wheeler County's best turkey hunting can be found south of Highway 26 and east and west of Highway 207.

If your turkey hunting takes you to Morrow County, the Umatilla National Forest, southeast of Heppner, is producing some gobblers.

Umatilla County has some turkey hunting near Pendleton, and near Meacham and Ukiah in the National Forest. Union County's hunters can find turkeys northwest of Elgin in the Grande Ronde watershed.

In Wallowa County, turkey numbers are on the rise near Enterprise and in the Sled Springs and Chesnimnus Units in the northeast corner.

Union County has its share of birds. You don't have to go far out of La Grande to find them. Pay special attention to the Mt. Emily area.

Baker County is becoming well known for turkey hunting. Good bets are west of Baker City and Haines. The area around Halfway is becoming another gobbler hotspot.

Hunters have reported seeing flocks south of the middle fork of the John Day in the Malheur National Forest, and from Dayville to Prairie City along Highway 26.

Malheur and Harney Counties have limited turkey hunting. Best bet would be to hunt north of Burns.

East of the Cascades, the best turkey habitat is often on public ground. It is important to know the boundaries. Study BLM and Forest Service maps before you go.

FALL TURKEY
Thanksgiving Turkey: Go Gunning for Your Groceries

The National Turkey Federation, a poultry industry advocacy group, tells us that consumption of turkey meat has climbed to 17.6 pounds per person per year, up 108 percent since the early 1970s.

We take off our collective hats in salute to the turkey production industry for their efficiency at producing poultry and selling it to us. And then we put our hats back on. We can get our own turkey, thank you.

In our family, we try to keep the menu wild and in a lot of cases, we end up saving money. In the interests of research, we procured a farm-raised bird at the grocery store. Said turkey, which weighed in at 12 pounds ready-to-cook, cost $14.23. $1.19 per pound.

That was a bit of a reality check. One wild turkey cost me, with meals and fuel figured in, at least $8 per pound and a two-week rash of poison oak. On the positive side, that hen with nearly an eight-inch beard, was one of the best-eating turkeys I have ever had. And the bagging of that bird made a way better story than the manner in which we obtained our research bird.

Gary Lewis used a muzzleloading shotgun on this fall hunt near Roseburg.

It turns out that organic, free-range and locally grown turkeys can bring between $5 and $9 a pound. That puts my most recent wild turkey hunt expenditure on the high side of average.

Most people think of hunting wild turkeys in the spring, but Oregon has a fall season. If you're shopping for *Meleagris gallopavo*, you are going to need a fall turkey tag.

The Trask, Willamette, Santiam, Stott Mountain, Alsea, McKenzie, Siuslaw, Indigo, Dixon, Melrose, Tioga, Sixes, Powers, Chetco, Applegate, Evans Creek and Rogue units are open for the general season hunt. Tags are sold on a first-come, first-served basis. The daily bag limit is one turkey of either sex and hunters may take two turkeys for the season.

A controlled fall turkey hunt takes place in the White River, Baker, Blue Mountain, Grand Ronde and Wallowa districts. Pick up a copy of the Oregon Game Bird Regulations for details.

This time of year, the birds are in good sized groups. Hens make up the largest bunches. Young jakes run together and the bigger toms keep to themselves, in bands of eight to ten.

Pay the most attention to river bottoms near stands of oak. Turkeys like to eat acorns, but they also prospect in open meadows on grubs, worms and insects. In ranchland, the turkeys fatten up around sheep and cattle feeders, where they scavenge spilled corn and grain.

Hens average eight to ten pounds. For the best value per pound, hold out for a gobbler, which can run between 14 and 25 pounds.

Fall turkeys will come to a call, but ambush tactics seem to pay off better at this time of year. Spot and stalk, or set up a blind and let them come to you.

A wild turkey hunt can come with exercise you won't get in the frozen food aisle. One rainy December day, I climbed a ridge and tucked between a fence post and an oak tree to wait while a flock of shiny toms headed my way.

The fence ran the tree line, down into little washes and up grassy slopes. The birds would have to cover almost 250 yards to get from where I'd last seen them to within range of my muzzleloader.

I steadied the smoothbore against the tree and snugged the butt into my shoulder. With my cheek against the wood, I laid my finger along the outside of the trigger guard, aware of two sounds: the squawks of the turkeys, close now, and the pounding of my heart.

The first gobbler crested the rise, a boss tom with an eight-inch beard. Hit, the bird went down and then got up before I had time to reload. I sprinted over 300 yards, reloading on the run, to catch it at the creek bottom. That turkey harvest translated to about 11 pounds RTC and $5 per pound in expenses. Not to mention what I saved on a gym membership.

Shop for your turkey with a shotgun this holiday season. You'll get a chance at a bird as organic as organic gets. Lean, free-range, with no added hormones or antibiotics. It's a bird that tastes as good, or better, than any frozen fowl.

The story tells better around the table than a jaunt through the frozen foods aisle. If you pick up a rash, the scratching will help you burn calories for a couple of weeks after the big dinner.

SHOT SELECTION GUIDE FOR WATERFOWL, UPLAND BIRDS, RABBITS AND SQUIRRELS

Game	Gauge	Lead shot	Non-toxic	Steel
Ducks	10,12,16,20	not legal	#2-#6	1-#6
Geese	10,12	not legal	BB-#4	#2-T
Snipe	12-28,.410	#7-#9	#7-#9	#7
Doves	12-28	#7-#9	#7-#9	#7
Quail	12-28	#6-#8	#7-#9	#5-#7
Chukar and Hungarian Partridge	12-28	#4-#8	#7-#9	#4-#7
Ruffed and Blue Grouse	12-28	#4-#8	#7-#9	#4-#7
Pheasant	12-28	#3-#6	#7-#9	#3-#6
Wild Turkey	12-20	BB-#6	#7-#9	#3-#5
Cottontail Rabbits	12-28,.410	#4-#6	#2-#4	#4
Jackrabbits	12-20	#4	#2-#4	#2
Western Gray Squirrel	12-28,.410	#6	#2-#4	#4

Cowboy Action Shooting is a great family, couples or buddy sport, from ages 12 to over 85! Our friendly Pistoleros offer you quallified training and great support in a fun and safe environment.
SASS - Club of the Year - 2009

www.hrp-sass.com

THE HORSE RIDGE PISTOLEROS
COME SHOOT WITH US IN THE EXCITING SPORT OF COWBOY ACTION SHOOTING.

Texas Jack Morales
541.420.3955

Big Casino
541.389.2342

SMALL GAME - GROUND SQUIRRELS

GROUND SQUIRRELS

Make a Hole in One!

*I*n the spring, when the snows recede and shoots of new green grass show among last year's stalks, the thoughts of thousands of Oregon sportsmen turn to the same thing. Golf!

They'll don a polo shirt, funny pants, a driving glove and white shoes, then head to the links. The green of the grass, the puffy clouds against a blue sky and a little white ball driven from tee to green for 18 holes. Most duffers will be happy to shoot par on a single hole, but a few lucky players will hit a hole-in-one.

Out on the dry side of the state, there are plenty of golf courses, especially in places like Bend, Eagle Crest, The Running Y Ranch, Redmond and Sunriver. But not far away, on green fields of alfalfa from the Columbia to California and from the Cascades east to the Snake and the Steens, you can drive a bullet instead of a ball. Instead of pulling out your seven-iron, reach for your shooting iron.

Charlie Lake, with a customized Ruger 10/22, takes aim on a pivot rest in Lake County.

GROUND SQUIRRELS

The Belding's ground squirrel is a short-haired, thin-tailed critter with a taste for alfalfa, subterranean cover and a penchant for procreation. In a large colony of squirrels, you'll see mounds of earth heaped up at the entrance to the den and trails leading hither and yon into the crops.

Burns resident, outfitter Justin Aamodt has made it his business to find solutions for ranchers beset by the little critters. "They tunnel and weaken the soil, he said, "and make mounds that cover potential crops. Often, the mounds are high

Certified Organic

A hunter who knocks on a rancher's or a farmer's door to ask for permission to shoot ground squirrels can create a win-win-win situation for landowner, hunter and consumer.

One day, as I was leaving for Burns and beyond, a thank-you note showed up in the mail from a landowner whose property I'd hunted a couple of weeks before. He explained how much damage the varmints had done to his crops and how necessary it was to keep them under control if he expected to take any orchard grass to market.

Producing a crop that was certified organic, he could not use chemicals to control the critters. Populations of ground squirrels, absent well-drained fields and major food sources, don't usually grow out of balance. But to a rancher or a farmer, making a living on the land, colonies of sage rats can cause no end of trouble.

In the past, poisons were often employed to keep the diggers in check, but if a farmer wants to maintain a certified organic status, the best option is a hunter with a rifle.

enough that when the rancher cuts his alfalfa, the dirt and rocks can dull or break the blades on his machines."

Safety-conscious hunters, who pick up their brass and don't drive on crop fields, can help control rodents so that landowners won't choose to resort to poisons.

One rancher had so many squirrels living on his grain that he plowed up his fields to get rid of them, missing two cuttings of alfalfa and the sale of 600 bales.

However, the varmints are a part of the food chain and populations shouldn't be eradicated. Safety-conscious hunters, who pick up their brass and don't drive on crop fields, can help control rodents so that landowners won't choose to resort to poisons.

A variable scope is a big help and shooting sticks can make the difference when every little bit of accuracy counts. Often the quarry is almost hidden behind a mound of dirt, leaving you a target no bigger than a silver dollar.

Binoculars can help the spotter direct shots. For the young shooter, looking forward to his or her first big game season, the practice is invaluable.

ALFALFA ARSENAL Many shooters have turned to the .17 HMR. It is quiet compared to most centerfire rifles, but it can reach well beyond the range of the .22 rimfire. You can see the impact. There's no recoil and it's accurate out to 200 yards. The only trouble with these light bullets is that they're vul-

Permission to Hunt

Property owners are often happy to let you shoot, but permission must be obtained. Keep in mind that well-traveled highways carry the most hunters and access might be easier to find off the beaten path. Establish relationships with landowners prior to the hunt or contact an outfitter for a guided shoot on private ground.

Once you've found a place to hunt, make yourself a welcome guest. Pick up your empty brass and litter left by other shooters. When negotiating the fields in your four-wheel drive, don't leave the ranch roads. If you drive over the landowner's crops you won't be invited back.

nerable to the effects of a stiff breeze.

Moving up to a centerfire can help you buck the wind. For something different, try the .204 Ruger. A .223 or a .22-.250 pushing a 40-grain Ballistic Tip can extend your reach

when a badger emerges on a faraway field.

Whatever hardware you choose, there are diggers of all types on eastern Oregon's ranchlands and public lands. Don't let your poor score on the golf course get you down. Go out and make a hole-in-one.

> **Protected Species**
>
> A SMALL GAME HUNT IS A GOOD TIME TO TEACH A NOVICE THE DIFFERENCE BETWEEN LEGAL SMALL GAME AND PROTECTED SPECIES. HUNTERS SHOULD AVOID SHOOTING PINE SQUIRRELS, GOLDEN-MANTLED GROUND SQUIRRELS AND CHIPMUNKS, WHICH ARE PROTECTED BY LAW.

A seated shot can be made steadier by resting an elbow against one or both knees.

Jennifer Lewis takes aim with a CZ rimfire, chambered for .17 HMR. The diminutive round has become a favorite of small game hunters from east to west.

ROCKCHUCKS

Yellow-bellied marmot, whistle pig, whatever you call him, a rockchuck provides big game hunting excitement in a small package. Growing as large as 10 pounds or more, these furry rodents make their home in rocky outcroppings or rock piles, leaving them only to graze on nearby vegetation.

They live in small groups and are kept in check by hawks, coyotes, foxes, and bobcats. But give them an alfalfa field and the marmot armies will tunnel, weaken irrigation dams and multiply rapidly, decimating crops, and competing with cattle and horses for food.

Rockchucks like to graze in the open, but prefer borders for their dens. Fence lines or pasture boundaries offer the raised mounds of earth that rockchucks use for visibility and proximity to forage.

Wonder if rockchucks are nearby? You can find their droppings on rockpiles and large holes in the pasture. Holes big enough that a galloping horse can put a foot down one and break a leg.

Getting within range is the hard part. As when hunting larger animals, check the wind before beginning your stalk. Spending time afield in the spring is a good way to sharpen your shooting skills for fall seasons, whether you shoot a handgun, rifle, bow, or muzzleloader.

Whatever you bring, hunt as a team. Two hunters working together can take turns with the spot and the stalk; can alternate shooting and calling the shots.

Binoculars are essential for long-range spotting. Getting close is the hard part. As with larger animals, check the wind before beginning your stalk. Camouflage clothing will help you blend into your environment while you wait for the shot.

April and May are prime months to ambush big chucks in the growing alfalfa. By mid-June, the grass and crops may be too tall to see them on the ground. In the summer the best bet is to spot and stalk rockchucks up in the rimrocks and canyons that feed down into agricultural lands.

While rockchucks can be found at high elevations in the Cascades, concentrations of the animals can be found from north central Oregon south through Klamath Falls and east to the Idaho border. Hunters will find the most animals on private land, but good hunting can be found wherever a rockchuck can make a living on fresh green grass and forbs adjacent to broken rocky habitat. For the best opportunities, establish relationships with landowners prior to the hunt, or contact an outfitter that offers springtime hunts on private land.

For big game practice on a small scale, head east of the Cascades from Madras south to Klamath Falls, and hunt rockchucks, also called yellow-bellied marmots, in and around agricultural land. April, May and June offer prime shooting.

Landowners are often happy to let you shoot, but permission must be obtained.

WESTERN GRAY SQUIRREL

Sciurus griseus, the western gray squirrel, is bluish-gray or silver-gray in appearance. Its underbelly is generally white as are the ends of the guard hairs in the tail, lending a frosted or silver look to the tail.

Because the squirrel can provide a good meal for hawks, owls, weasels, minks, bobcats, foxes, coyotes or humans, he must be alert at all times, whether on the ground or high in a tree. Frightened, he takes to the closest tree, using its trunk to shield him from danger. With a predator close behind, he jumps from the branches of one tree to the next, using branches and trunks and foliage to keep out of view.

For the regulations governing the western gray squirrel, turn to the Oregon Big Game Regulations.

Alternately, he may freeze and wait for danger to pass, laying his belly against the bark, tense, claws locked, ready to run.

To find squirrels in abundance, look to their food sources. Acorns from oak trees and pine nuts from pine trees are favorites. In the spring, they eat the buds of new growth on the branches of trees. In the fall, they may find apples in old orchards. They need water and will take it several times a day when it is available.

During stormy weather the squirrels hole up, but they don't hibernate like bears or rockchucks. They require food for the winter months and so spend much of the autumn months gathering a supply against cold weather.

Look for stands of oak trees or other nut-producing trees. An old apple orchard close to timberlands may also produce good hunting.

The best time of day for hunting squirrels is in the early morning, from when the dawn's first light is warming the tops of the trees till about ten o'clock.

Watch the water sources at mid-morning and again in mid-afternoon. Squirrels will generally stay close to their nests during the warmer part of the day and start feeding again in the evening.

Listen and watch more than you walk for the slightest movement, the twitch of an ear, the flick of a tail, the shine of an eye. Listen for the cutting of teeth on nuts or the skittering of claws on bark.

The stand hunter finds a patch of cover with good feed and access to water. Prowling carefully through the trees, he locates discarded nut shells or chewed pine cones or the cores of apples. Taking a position, leaning back against a tree, the hunter watches and waits.

A .22 rimfire rifle or handgun loaded with solid point ammunition is good squirrel medicine. Shots at squirrels are generally taken at less than 50 yards. A .410 shotgun loaded with No. 6 shot is the favored load for scatter-gunners. This is also the weapon of choice for the walking hunter whose targets will likely be leaping from tree to tree or running along the ground.

For the tremendous hunting opportunity and the education that squirrel hunting provides, you can't beat the western gray squirrel.

West of the Cascades, the season is liberal with squirrel hunting available in all Westside units. In a portion of the Rogue unit, south of the Rogue River and the South Fork of the Rogue and north of Highway 140, there is no bag limit or closed season at all.

East of the Cascades, the White River and Hood units support western gray squirrel hunting. Check the Oregon Big Game Regulations for season dates and bag limits. ◾

COTTONTAIL AND JACKRABBIT

COTTONTAILS

Rabbits don't require a lot to thrive: A little food, water, shelter and escape cover. They can find everything they need in a few acres of ground. Best of all, rabbits may be hunted close to home.

Cottontails breed in the spring and summer, producing up to eight litters, each with three to six young. They prefer brushy edges and woodlots, but can live almost anywhere with the exception of dense forests. They eat practically any type of green plant. When green vegetation dies back, they switch to twigs and bark.

Rabbits start feeding before dawn and continue for two or three hours and resume feeding at sunset. They move about most on calm, sunny days. Rain or wind drives them into heavy cover.

A cottontail spends most of the day sitting in a *form*, a shallow depression in grass or snow. The grass eventually wears away, or the snow melts down and compacts. Often a form is concealed by overhanging grass or other type of overhead cover.

Rabbits use their superb hearing to sense impending danger. To escape, they bolt away on established travel lanes. Cottontails run in an elusive, zigzag pattern, but their speed is not as fast as a jackrabbit. They normally run 12 to 15 mph, but can reach 20 mph.

Normally, cottontails will not run far. Rather than run straight away, a rabbit will circle so it can stay in familiar territory. When frightened, it will often slip into a woodchuck burrow or brush pile.

You can bag some cottontails by walking through cover, looking for rabbits in their forms. Upland bird hunters flush rabbits by moving in typical walk-and-wait fashion. Like deer, a cottontail becomes nervous when a nearby hunter stands motionless, and will often bound from its resting spot.

Populations of cottontails and jackrabbits are prone to fluctuation. Although they are solitary by nature, large groups of rabbits may be found together when food sources are concentrated.

Hunting with dogs offers an interesting and effective alternative. Most hunters use slow-moving hounds, like beagles and bassets. When the dogs get close, the cottontail begins moving in a large circle and will eventually pass within shooting range of the hunter. Almost any dog will chase cottontails, but if it works too fast, the rabbit will dash under a brush pile or down a hole.

Rabbits may contract a bacterial disease called tularemia, which causes them to behave listlessly and eventually kills them. But the disease is rare. One researcher found it in only 2 of 12,000 rabbits he examined. Nevertheless, refrain from shooting rabbits that move slowly or otherwise behave unusually. Tularemia can be transmitted to humans who eat or handle the flesh of infected animals.

To hit zigzagging cottontails, most hunters use shotguns with modified or improved cylinder chokes, and No. 6 shot. But when rabbits are in their forms or feeding in the open, reach for a .22 rifle.

JACKRABBITS

The home range of the black-tailed jackrabbit is in low-lying semi-desert. Jackrabbits (which are technically hares, not rabbits) may also be found in typical cottontail country and around tree plantations in more temperate climates. Night feeders, jackrabbits are best hunted in the low light of early morning and in the evening. Landowners are often happy to allow hunting to keep populations from destroying valuable alfalfa and other crops.

The black-tailed jackrabbit grows to a length of about 24 inches, and adults weigh between one pound and two pounds. They can reach speeds of up to 35 mph, and can leap up to 5 yards in a single jump.

Although they are largely solitary animals, they may be found in large groups at certain times of the year, especially when feeding on a plot of alfalfa.

One of the most productive methods for hunting jack rabbits is the drive. A group of three to five hunters works the best. Hunters walk in a line through good rabbit habitat, spread out with about ten yards in between. Rimfire rifles and 20-gauge shotguns are the preferred tools. Rabbits will be pushed out ahead of the group or hold tight to run the opposite direction after the drive has moved past.

For safety's sake, high-visibility blaze orange is essential on these hunts, and the group leader should ensure that the line stays intact.

When flushed, jackrabbits zig and zag, putting brush and distance between the hunter and hunted. Unlike cottontails, jackrabbits don't often circle back; they're headed for the horizon. Be ready, because you will probably not get another chance.

A day spent walking after jackrabbits is a good way to sharpen rifle skills for upcoming big game hunts.

West of the Cascades, hunt rabbits in tree plantations and swamps. Pay special attention to agricultural lands and brushpiles. Always secure permission to hunt on private lands. East of the Cascades, hunt the grasslands, sagebrush and rimrock areas adjacent to ag lands or reliable water sources. In eastern Oregon, the best bets are on or around private land, close to water sources and fields of alfalfa.

RACCOON AND BADGER

RACCOON

Equipped with needle-sharp teeth and a quick temper, the raccoon is a fighter and a challenge to the houndsman/hunter. They may run for miles and when cornered, can kill or maim hunting dogs twice their size.

Hardwood forests and marshy lowlands near water make good raccoon habitat. Berries, fruits, nuts, frogs, crayfish and insects are all on the menu, but sweet corn is a favorite.

An adult raccoon may travel up to five miles on its nightly feeding rounds, especially in warm weather. During the day they often den up in hollow trees. But they may bed in the tall vegetation along the edge of a marsh, in a culvert, or in the ground burrow of another animal. Raccoon frequently use different dens or beds on successive days. They den up for a period after heavy snow; in cold climates they may hibernate.

Raccoon have excellent hearing and good eyesight. They can run up to 15 mph and are good swimmers. The vast majority of hunting them is done with hounds, especially Walkers, black-and-tans and red-bones. Tracking is easiest on damp, cool nights with a slight breeze. Some dogs can pick up a cold trail, making it possible to hunt in daylight.

When pursued by dogs, raccoon usually run in large circles, crawling in and out of holes and climbing up and down trees to lose the dogs. They may jump to the ground from as high as 50 feet and scurry away unharmed. They will stay in a tree only when the hounds get so close that other avenues of escape are impossible.

Early in the season you may be able to call a raccoon. After dark, take a stand along a streambank, lakeshore, or cornfield. Use calls to imitate an injured bird or rabbit.

Most raccoon hunters use .22 rifles, although some prefer 20 gauge shotguns with No. 6 or 7-1/2 shot. Where legal, a few hunters use small-caliber handguns.

BADGER

The badger, a member of the weasel family, is on the prowl wherever other ground-dwelling varmints are abundant. Small rodents, snakes, birds, insects and eggs are on the daily menu of this solitary animal.

A male badger, which can weigh up to 20 pounds or more, will range far and wide, covering a large territory that may take in a square mile of ground or much more, depending on the habitat. It is a largely nocturnal animal, but in areas of little human activity, you might see a badger during daylight hours.

For a badger, home is wherever it happens to be when it's time to rest. It will simply dig a burrow and crawl inside. In less than a minute, it can be underground. For this reason, if you've found a badger's territory, you will find dozens of empty holes in banks close to water sources and squirrel colonies.

Many badgers are taken each year by ground squirrel hunters. Your best opportunity will be in the morning before the shooting starts. Keep an eye out for a badger on the move, headed for its hole.

Badgers will respond to a call, but are not likely to travel far to reach the caller. Successful badger hunters stay on the move until a badger is spotted at long range then set up to call.

When using a call, focus on sounds made by easily-caught ground dwellers like ground squirrels. A squirrel, prairie dog or woodpecker in distress may bring a badger on the run.

COYOTES

Mr. Coyote - Don't Call Him Late for Dinner

Scientists classify the coyote under the order *Carnivora* in the family *Canidae*. *Canis latrans* has been called the brush wolf and the prairie wolf. Some folks call them song dogs and others call them yodelers. The Aztecs called them coyotl. Ranchers call them trouble at calving time.

When there is snow on the ground, you can call them hungry.

We headed east and south into the junipers and sagebrush. An inch of grainy white stuff lay like a blanket on the ground. Tracks laced the landscape. Almost every deer trail had a coyote print that ran parallel. It looked like the dogs were hunting in packs.

"I told you there were a lot of coyotes here," Bob Williams said.

He was right about that. Seldom have I seen such a concentration of coyote activity. A few minutes later, we saw the reason why. Mule deer. A herd of does bounced away through the junipers.

I guessed that a fawn distress call would bring a coyote within range of my semi-auto .223 or Bob's .243. I dialed the Trijicon down to 3x. Action was likely to be up close and personal.

We set up the FoxPro caller and a decoy about 40 yards out. Robbie, Bob's son saw the first coyote, 30 seconds into the set. But Robbie wasn't carrying a gun. I made sure that he sat right next to his dad on the second set.

This time a coyote crossed behind the decoy then went behind a juniper. A minute later, he was in our laps. But sometimes close is too close. That one got away.

On the third set, we had company in less than three minutes. At least two showed on the horizon, but I saw coyote ears above the sage, about 60 yards away, behind the decoy. And then the ears began a quick exit stage left.

There. A glimpse as it flashed through sagebrush. I swung the Trijicon triangle and squeezed the trigger as the dog passed through an opening. One down.

We saw no coyotes on the fourth set, but the fifth set paid off. This time, we used mouth calls for a jackrabbit/cottontail duet, and took up perches in a couple of juniper trees to gain elevation and watch for free-loading furbearers. In seven minutes, we had another inbound coyote dash headlong for dinner. I missed the first shot (incoming) at 15 yards and saw the dog skid and make a quick right turn. I picked it up again, going away, and stopped it.

Some callers use confidence decoys to lure the coyotes in. Jack rabbit, cottontail, bird and fawn decoys give the coyote something to look at as it approaches.

SCOUTING FOR COYOTES

The coyote has become educated about how to live around people. Even within the city limits of Portland, Eugene, Salem and Medford, coyotes prowl the golf courses and fields in search of their prey. In the suburbs, residents complain about the coyotes that roam at will, eating from dog food dishes and garbage cans or picking up unsuspecting dogs and cats.

A good place to hunt coyotes is wherever they can find their principal foods. Fields, meadows and prairies are full of mice; brushy draws hold rabbits and upland birds. Wherever there are antelope or deer there will be coyotes close by. In the spring when ungulates are giving birth to their young a fawn-in-distress call can draw in predators.

When you find an area that has all the right coyote foods, look for sign. Droppings are about the same size as a dog's of similar size but the scat will be small and twisted on the end. It will contain undigested bits of whatever the animal has been feeding on. Deer hair, bits of rabbit and mouse fur and even berries are found in coyote droppings.

An adult coyote stands less than 24 inches tall and varies in color from whitish-gray to brown with sometimes a reddish cast to its pelt. Ears and nose appear long and pointed, in relation to the size of its head. It weighs between 20 and 50 pounds and can be identified by a thick, bushy tail, which it often holds low to the ground. He is an extremely lean, fast animal that may reach speeds up to 43 mph.

The coyote pelt is best after the first snows and a tanned pelt or a coyote rug makes a fine trophy to remember a successful hunt.

CALLING COYOTES A fawn-in-distress or a dying rabbit predator call costs only a few dollars and can be easily mastered. Electronic calls with remote controls and motorized decoys cost more, but provide a way for the hunter to watch the call from a distance.

Look for edge habitat where agricultural lands butt up against sagebrush and junipers. Canyons and dry washes are like highways for coyotes. A pair or a trio will run the length of a wash, on the prowl for rabbits or deer, teamed up for the chase.

Set up in front of a bush or a tree to break up your outline and post a partner to keep watch in another direction. Often, a coyote circles to catch the scent stream before charging in.

A shot at a coyote might be taken as close as ten feet or as far out as 300 yards. A good coyote gun should be able to accommodate either circumstance.

Coyotes perform a valuable function, keeping rodent and rabbit populations in check. However, as coyote populations increase they can put a severe dent in the numbers of deer and antelope herds.

In cattle country, coyotes are never far away.

A coyote may respond anytime of day, but the first two hours in the day and the last two hours of light are the best times for calling.

The coyote knows the sound of a rabbit or a rodent in distress means an easy meal, if it can take the prey away from whatever is killing it. This is why sometimes a dominant coyote will come right in while a younger dog might be hesitant.

Put fright and pain in the calling. The first sounds a rabbit makes when it is captured are a series of squalls which then become gasping cries. If the predator shifts its grip then the squalls might come again.

Study the land and determine likely approaches a coyote might make. The wind is of paramount importance. Situate yourself downwind from where the coyote is likely to be. Place hunting partners up to 50 yards away from the caller.

Wear full camouflage, gloves and a facemask. But don't let the facemask break up your peripheral vision – you're going to need it. A flick of a tail, a pair of ears above the tops of the grass, a flash of fur in the sage, a bird spooked from a bush – all these could be clues a dog is coming in. Keep all movement to a minimum. As coyotes approach they will be zeroed in on the location of the caller.

Call in one location for at least 20 minutes.

Depending on the topography you might need only move a quarter of a mile before calling again.

Start with a subtle cry, sustained for about 30 seconds. Wait two minutes then increase the volume. Call for about 30 seconds at a time and then go silent for about two minutes. If you're imitating a rabbit or a fawn in distress, remember that these animals have small lung capacity and cries are likely to be of short duration. Consider using a bird in distress call instead, in areas where the dogs are likely to have experience with camo-clad rabbit impostors.

For a dedicated coyote rifle, the best choice might be one of the flat-shooting .22 centerfires or a 6mm or .243. Beyond these, any rifle a big-game hunter is proficient with is the perfect choice for coyotes.

When the coyote is likely to come in close, a shotgun is ideal. Use a load with sufficient knockdown power in the range between No. 2s and 00 buckshot.

Yotey, prairie wolf, yodel-dog – call him what you like, but don't call him late for dinner. ◼

This coyote was surprised from its bed on the side of a butte.

Coyotes are more active when snow is on the ground. Cold weather speeds up metabolisms and the predator becomes more vulnerable to the sound of its prey in distress.

On a call set for coyotes, set up in front of a bush to break up your outline.

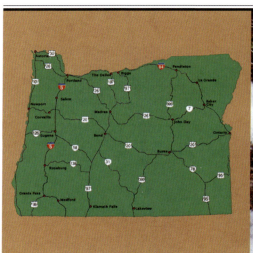

BOBCAT
By Duane Dungannon

I was shocked. The geese were gone. What could have spooked them?

My son Tyler and I had seen the honkers lounging lakeside near a rocky jetty and made a wide circle and a stealthy stalk to ambush the birds at close range. But when we crested the jetty, shotguns ready for a surprise attack, the real surprise was that we now had the lake to ourselves – or so we thought.

We scratched our heads as we headed back to the truck. Then a movement to my left caught my eye. Could it be? It was one of those things you didn't want to say you thought you saw in case you were wrong; you know your kids will never let you hear the end of it.

Then there it was – standing on a rock, silhouetted against the Lake County sky – an eastern Oregon bobcat big enough that he wasn't backing down from anyone or anything.

Following a frustrating fall season of big game hunting, this was the winter I had decided to get serious about predator hunting. I had bought my Oregon furbearer hunting license and bobcat harvest card and would start doing some hardcore calling as soon as waterfowl season ended.

I had never intended to take my first bobcat while bird hunting, so I was still a little incredulous this was really happening as I leveled the side-by-side goose gun loaded with steel BB. I touched the trigger, and the big eastern Oregon tom I had always wanted was mine.

Taxidermist Lance Podolski mounted that bobcat leaping at a rooster sage grouse I had taken earlier that fall in Malheur County. It's easily the favorite mount of all who visit my home.

Oregon is home to a remarkable number of bobcats, more than one would ever guess roamed the state based on the number of cats the average hunter observes in broad daylight. A study at Douglas County's North Bank Habitat Area determined that bobcats are the leading cause of deer fawn mortality in the area. On one hunt with Tyler at North Bank, we saw two bobcats there in one weekend. When you see two bobcats in two days, you can be confident there are many more bobcats prowling around that you don't ever see.

Oregon's bobcat season typically opens at the start of December and runs through the end of February. A furbearer hunting license and bobcat harvest card are required. Bag limits are subject to change, but have traditionally been much more liberal in western Oregon than on the east side of the Cascades. The trade-off is that the eastern Oregon cats are bigger, and their pelts are considered more desirable.

Consult the Oregon Furbearer Trapping and Hunting Regulations for current season dates, license requirements and bag limits.

There are three methods for hunting bobcat in Oregon: hound hunting, predator calling and dumb luck.

While dumb luck worked for me, I don't recommend it. Given the number of incidental encounters you can expect, it's likely you will invest hundreds of dollars in licenses and harvest cards before you ever set your sights on a bobcat.

Since the 1994 passage of Measure 18, which banned the use of hounds for hunting bear and cougar in Oregon, bobcats have become the main quarry of houndsmen in the state. If you don't own hounds or know someone who does, your best bet is to hire a guide.

Hiring the services of a capable guide can get expensive, but you stand a good chance of being successful in your hunt, and at the very least, you can expect to get in on some wild chases.

Snow not only reveals the tracks of bobcats, it holds the scent in the tracks, making it easier for hounds to follow the trail. A hound hunt for bobcats in a winter wonderland can be an exhilarating – albeit exhausting – action adventure.

Female bobcats are smaller than the males, and you may tree several cats before you find the big tom you want.

If chasing dogs that are chasing cats all over a mountainside in knee-deep snow isn't for you, you may find it preferable to simply sit tight and call the cats to you instead. Winter is prime time for cat calling as well, not only because pelts are in premium condition, but also because many of their primary prey animals have either flown south for the winter or denned up underground for a long winter's nap.

The popularity of predator hunting has increased dramatically in recent years, and as a result, more predator calling products are available than ever before. A variety of calls are preferred, including electronic calls that can be very effective, particularly when used in combination with a decoy.

Decoys serve two key purposes: they attract predators to your setup, and they divert the attention of the animal away from the hunter. The cheapest decoys aren't much more than a simple stuffed animal, while the more elaborate ones use battery power to create eye-catching movement that can make a bobcat forget its inhibitions and come running for dinner.

Good camouflage is essential, and should include a facemask or face paint. Pay particular attention to wind direction, and set up where you can get a clear shot at a cat approaching from downwind.

Finally, remember that bobcats are not the only hungry predators looking for a hot meal on a cold day. While bears aren't very active during bobcat season, you may well attract coyotes, fox and even cougars to your setup, so it's a good idea to hunt with a partner who literally has your back covered. ∎

Oregon Furbearer Trapping and Hunting Regulations are available at the nearest office of the Oregon Department of Fish and Wildlife.

Check the current regulations before going afield. Hunters are required to possess a Resident Hunting License for Furbearers and a Bobcat Record Card. *Photo courtesy Duane Dungannon*

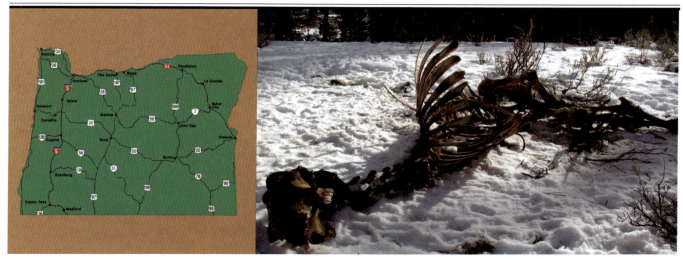

MOUNTAIN LION

Afternoon sunlight filtered down through the pine needles. Rich Newton, of Albany, and his wife, Kathy, had returned to camp to let their dog out for a walk and a dip in the lake. Headed up the trail without their bows, the Newtons let the dog lead the way.

When she left the trail, they followed. In 15 yards, they came to a dead elk, a yearling cow, with puncture wounds on her shoulders and in the back of her neck. A cougar had killed her and had neither fed on the animal, nor buried it. Nearby, Newton found the impact point where the cat had hit the elk and driven it to the ground. Something had scared the cat away, but there was a good chance he was coming back.

Newton looked around and noticed a rock the size of a Volkswagen about 30 yards from the kill. A plan began to take shape. "Kathy," he said, "I'm going to come back and wait for that cougar."

Back at camp, Newton showered and used Dead Downwind Scent Killer on his clothes. He hiked back to within a couple of hundred yards of the kill then reapplied the Scent Killer.

When he reached the rock, it was 5:00pm. Four hours of daylight left. He nocked an arrow then took out his Bible and began to read.

An hour passed and a doe walked directly downwind of Newton. When he next checked his watch, two hours had passed. 7:00pm. Shadows grew longer and the pink and rose of evening began to fill the sky. "I forgot why I was there," Newton said later. "That's when I heard the crash."

"I eased around the rock and the cat was broadside to me. He was pouncing on the elk and coming down really hard, really intense. I moved my release hand not more than five inches to the nock and he saw me and froze."

Broadside at 30 yards.

The cat snapped his tail. "I made the decision, I'm pulling."

The big cat turned face-on toward Newton and stepped off the rock. "He came down and his paw was huge. The skin around the paw folded down around the foot, muffling the sound. He was locked on me like he had radar. Intent. Looking at my chest. I pulled and brought my pins down."

The cat had taken five steps, so Newton split the distance, calculating a 25-yard shot. When the pin settled, he tickled the release and buried the shaft deep into the cat's chest.

Hit, the cat screamed and jumped "two or three feet in the air and turned and crossed the hiking trail."

Newton began to shake, his calm shattered. "There was a flow of blood as wide as the palm of my hand. I knew this cat was not going to go far."

His dog led Rich Newton, of Albany, OR, to a freshly killed cow elk. Newton read the sign and knew the cougar would be back. The cat yielded 92 pounds of meat back from the butcher. *Photo courtesy Rich Newton*

He nocked another arrow and followed to a tree with branches that hung all the way to the ground. "I was a yard away from it when he exploded from out of the other side of the tree."

When he had the nerve up to follow again, the blood trail led back to within 10 yards of the hiking path.

"That hiking trail was probably less than half the distance from camp to the lake. Fishermen walk right by that spot on their way in. My wife and I had seen a cougar just about every year for the last few years. The elk population there has really declined, especially in the last five years. If I didn't love the country so much, I would go somewhere else."

"I hadn't had any interest in killing a cougar or bear because it was going to take time away from elk hunting. But this was just a gift handed to me. I felt an obligation to hunt the animal."

Newton advises caution to other hunters who might stumble on a similar situation. "Everything was great until the sun went down. I just didn't think it through."

Newton didn't expect to fail, but now he says, he shudders to think what might have happened, had he missed that shot with the cat coming straight at him.

"Think about escape routes," he said. "And do you have a backup for your bow?"

Next stop was the Canyonville/John Day ODFW office. "The biologists were so enthusiastic about this cat. They know it was at least seven years old. He was missing a left front canine tooth and one claw on one of his paws. He had a noticeable scar on top of his head."

"The thing about a dominant male mountain lion," they told me, "is that it spends its whole life killing big game animals and when it isn't doing that, it is trying to kill any other animal it perceives as competition in its territory."

"That elk he killed was a yearling. He dragged it about 300 yards up over some rocks. It looked like a human being had gutted her with a cut straight like a knife."

"I got a real appreciation for the cat and the respect (the ODFW) people had for it. The day at the ODFW office was a well-spent day during my bow hunting season."

Consult the *Oregon Big Game Regulations* before hunting. It is illegal to take spotted kittens or to harvest a female with spotted kittens. Any cougar taken must be checked in at the nearest ODFW office within 72 hours of the kill. Fish and Wildlife requires that the hide, skull and proof of sex be checked in. If the cat is a female, the reproductive tract must be submitted as well.

Open seasons vary across the state. In some areas the big cats may be hunted year-round. Talk to ODFW biologists to find areas with high lion populations and then start talking to landowners. Lions are a real concern for many rural residents.

Oregon's lion population is growing. They pad the wilderness trails in the summer and follow deer down into the valleys and river canyons in the winter. Few hunters have seen him, but you can be certain, if you walk the high ridges in the fall or sit on a desert rimrock high above a river, a mountain lion has seen you. ■

Many cougars are taken incidental to hunts for other species. Mason Payer with a big cat he arrowed while hunting elk in eastern Oregon.

The cougar's principal prey species are deer and elk. To hunt the predator, keep tabs on its prey. The cat is never far away.

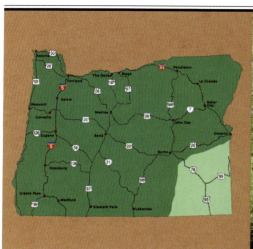

BLACK BEAR

Spring Black Bear Smarts
The Skill and Craft of Calling

The spring bear hunt is one of my favorite seasons, not because it is easy (it is not), but because the bears are there when the weather is warm, the grass is green and the buttercups are in bloom.

We spend an afternoon watching a long canyon and suddenly a bear appears on the far hillside. Time to make a decision, calculate the distance and the time required to get within range before daylight is gone. Inaction becomes intensity and a race against the sun.

Bears in the crosshairs, a mile out.

When they emerge from their winter dens, hungry bruins head straight for the creek and river valleys, taking advantage of succulent forage below the snowline. Grasses, grubs, wild onions, flowers, and the tender shoots of smaller trees and shrubs are the main food sources as the bears get their digestive juices flowing again.

When the foliage in the river bottoms dries out, the bears climb higher in search of goodies. This brings them into the open on green sunlit slopes where they may graze for hours, eating grass and turning over rocks in their search for insects and larvae.

Early in the season, hunting the stream bottoms can pay off. Later in the spring, go to the high country to find animals. Watch grassy slopes with binoculars or walk old logging roads.

Start with 8-power or 10-power binoculars. If you've located a good area and have found fresh tracks and other sign, be patient. If all the ingredients are there, the bear probably is too. Stay put, your bear could be bedded in the grass. You won't see him until he begins feeding again. This could mean staking out a promising area all day long. Patience pays off. The more time you can spend, glassing and watching, the less chance you'll have of spooking animals by moving too fast and spreading your scent.

DECISION TIME When the bear is spotted, it's decision time. Shoot? Make a stalk? Or call? This is when a rangefinder comes in handy. The traveling hunter is at a disadvantage when estimating distance. One quick laser calculation can tell you if you're within range or a stalk is in order.

Bears are very stalkable, but a lot of hunters make the mistake of underestimating their vision or hearing. They can pick up movement and sound and head for cover in a flash.

Scouting Tips

Down in the creek bottom, watch for patches of skunk cabbage. When the skunk cabbage blooms, it will produce a yellow stalk that resembles an ear of corn. When the 'corn' is ripe, watch the area closely.

Another food source bears focus on in the spring are the tops of young trees. This is another reason why old clearcuts can pay off with a look at a bear. Find a re-prod area, where seedlings have been planted to replace harvested timber. Such a spot can produce bear sightings for several years, until the trees are grown.

Guns and Loads for Black Bear

Bears are tough. A mortal wound will seldom put one down on the spot. You want to use a bullet that will break bone and do massive tissue damage. You want a hole large enough that the bear will continue to bleed.

Bear hair is longer than most hunters realize. It is capable of absorbing a lot of blood before a blood trail will start. For this reason alone, I now consider a .30-caliber bullet weighing 180 grains to be the minimum for a dedicated bear hunting rifle. A better choice would be a .32-caliber or larger punching out a 200 or 250-grain bullet. The 8mm Remington Magnum, .325 Winchester Short Magnum, .338 Winchester Magnum, .35 Whelen and .375 Ruger come to mind.

If shots under 100 yards are expected a lever-action rifle with open sights is a good choice. I would opt for the .358 Winchester, a hand-loaded .45-.70, or .450 Marlin.

It is also important to have a well-constructed bullet that you can rely upon. Nosler Partitions and AccuBonds are the industry standard for hunting dangerous game. You should choose a bullet with similar construction.

If there's one thing a hungry bear wants more than anything else, it's an easy meal. And he's used to taking food away from smaller predators. But bears are easily distracted. On the way in, he may stumble across something else he wants to eat. Keep the sound rolling to keep him on the move.

CALLING BLIND When you know there's a bear in the area and the terrain or foliage doesn't promise an easy spotting situation in the open, try the call. Focus on the setup and build the scenario. Pick a spot where visibility is better. Position a partner to watch the opposite direction. Sometimes bears, like other predators, will circle downwind to pick up the scent first.

Call with the wind in your favor and don't give the animal too many obstacles. I've had a bear swim a river and climb the bank to get to the call, but that was a dominant boar. Make the scenario promise an easy meal.

A call may bring a bear on the run, making the stalk unnecessary. In most areas, deer fawns, elk calves and ground squirrels are on the menu. A fawn or a rodent distress call can turn the balance in your favor.

Lee Van Tassell, my co-author on the book *Black Bear Hunting*, has tagged 28 black bears in several western states. Not a few of those bears were animals that responded to a call.

"Early in the season, I prefer to be on a north-facing slope, watching a south-facing slope," he said. "That's where you'll find the most mature foliage early in the spring."

Van Tassell prefers to call *after* he has spotted a bear.

"I'll use the call, especially in terrain where it takes half the day to make a cross-canyon stalk. I start with low volume for a short period of time, just to let them know something is out there. Then I pause and raise the volume."

The drawback to a mouth call in this situation is that the bear will pinpoint your position and come in head-on, looking for food and a fight. An electronic call, if it can be put into play with a minimum of trouble, can be positioned away from the hunter to allow for a quartering or a broadside shot.

The predator call – a fawn bawl or an injured squirrel – heightens the bear's awareness and raises the stakes.

When he heard the sound of a deer in distress, this bear plunged into the river and clambered up the bank. It was one of two bears that came to the call that September day.

And make it real. Use a cover scent and a fawn or rodent decoy.

Give him time. Depending on how far he's got to travel, you may see the bruin in a few minutes or an hour. Do your scouting first to make sure there are bears in the area, then keep the wind in your favor and your confidence high. Commit to spending an hour at each call set. Everything changes when the call is used. The predator may become aggressive, go passive, be curious or turn tail, depending on his hunger and place in the local bruin hierarchy. But calling works often enough that it is a viable option that can pressurize a lazy spring day and bring a bear into bow range.

Shooting 3-D targets is a good way to sharpen up for an archery hunt.

Black Bear in the Breaks

One of the best times of year to hunt bear is in the late summer. And one of the best places to find them is in northeast Oregon's Snake River, Imnaha and Chesnimnus Units.

Lee Van Tassell, Rick Jamison and Brian Clark with a big bruin taken from a clearcut.

When berries ripen in northeast Oregon, hunters have a chance to see high concentrations of black bear as they move down out of the mountains to put on their winter fat.

This corner of the state is characterized by open country with abundant edge habitat and transitions from tall timber to grassy slopes. It is home to mule deer, whitetail deer and elk – the black bear's natural prey. These Snake River country units are made to order for the spot-and-stalk hunter and for the hunter who prefers

Where to Hunt for Bear

Oregon's bear population is thought to be close to 30,000 animals, spread over approximately 40,000 square miles of habitat. The best bear concentrations are in southwest Oregon and up along the coast and in northeast Oregon.

Spring hunts are designed to keep bear populations at acceptable levels and are controlled by a lottery that limits hunters in each of the open units. Bag limit in the spring is one bear, except that it is unlawful to take cubs less than a year old, or sows with cubs.

The Department of Fish and Wildlife has adopted a mandatory check for all harvested bears. Biologists will remove a small premolar tooth and take some measurements. Hunters will be notified of the bear's age.

If you want to draw a tag the first year you apply, the best odds are west of the Cascades in the Wilson-Trask, North Cascades, Alsea-Stott Mountain, and Southwest Oregon hunts. The application deadline for the spring hunt is February 10. West of the Cascades, the season opens April 1. April 15 is the opener in most of the northeast hunts.

Hunt the middle of the season for the best chances of seeing bear; use the early season for scouting trips. Invest the time in places where you find fresh sign and be patient – the bears are there.

Spring bear hunting is growing in popularity, but the controlled seasons mean there are many places where a person can spend all day on a mountainside and never see another hunter. Watch the buttercups bloom and the hawks on the thermals. Look for deer, elk and turkeys in the meadows. You'll see a lot of rock bears and stump bears, but if you look long enough, one of those stumps will be a real bear, fresh from his den.

It will be a physically demanding hunt. Maybe there'll be a trophy at the end of it, maybe not. But the memories you bring back from bear country will be worth it all.

a predator call to bring a bruin on the run.

Early summer is the best time to hunt bears in mid-level habitat. The spring season finds the bears feeding on biscuitroot on the high, alpine meadows. When the hawthorn berry comes into season in August, bears migrate lower, out of the timber, onto the mountain benches and into the draws to feed.

Early in the morning is the best time to spot them moving around, going and coming from water. Watch the draws, but focus on the berry bushes.

The hawthorn is a shrubby tree that runs up and down the draws, usually pretty close to water. Sometimes you see them out on a bench and that's because there's a spring there or the water is close to the surface.

Orchards are also a draw early in the season. The old homesteads almost always have a fruit tree nearby. With the warm weather, bears need relief from the heat so north and east-facing timbered fingers are good places to look. We will see more bear activity in September than in August, most likely due to milder temps and shorter days.

PUTTING ON THE FEED BAG October marks the transition from the easy living of early fall to the cold weather to come. Snow in the high country signals the coming of winter and bears know that it's time to feed in a big way.

It's a simple principle. A skinny bear in November is a dead bear by May. In Oregon, the bear may sleep for five months and could lose up to thirty percent of its weight during that time. If he doesn't pack on the pounds in the last few weeks before heading to the den, he could starve to death.

When the weather cools and the nights get long, the bear instinctively knows he's running out of time. Depending on elevation and temperature, bears may go into the den in early November or as late as January. The bruin must put on a thick layer of fat. For the next five months, it serves as a reserve of nutrition and water and a blanket against the cold.

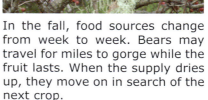

In the fall, food sources change from week to week. Bears may travel for miles to gorge while the fruit lasts. When the supply dries up, they move on in search of the next crop.

According to Leonard Erickson in the La Grande office of the Oregon Department of Fish and Wildlife, sows with cubs are the first to seek the den and settle in. The yearlings are next. In late October and early November, they should be localizing around their den site. And they're hungry. "They're still stuffing the tank as much as they can, while they can," he says.

During the late fall feeding binge, a black bear will consume up to 20,000 calories a day and put on as much

The place to eat in Central Oregon!

Good friends, Great food with a down home feel.

Taking the worry out of your event!
~Graduations
~Receptions
~Birthdays
~Meetings
~Reunions

The Ranch Hall

-Great dance floor
-Outdoor picnic area
-Seats 100+ people

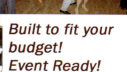

Built to fit your budget!
Event Ready!

541.548.7700
www.Coyote-Ranch.com   1368 S Hwy 97, Redmond, Oregon

as 30 pounds in a week. He naps for short periods of time and, if food is scarce, will travel up to a hundred miles to hit a big supply of groceries. At this time, he is focused on the feed and is not prone to wander in the typical fashion of a summer bear. He'll put on the feed bag, eat night and day, then turn around and head for home.

Lee Van Tassell has hunted black bears in Oregon, Washington, and Alaska for almost 30 years. The day we met we quickly discovered a mutual interest in black bears. Together, we wrote a book called *Black Bear Hunting* (2007, Creative Publishing International).

Van Tassell's insight into the world of the black bear comes through hundreds of hours spent behind the spotting scope and binoculars in both the spring and fall seasons.

"In October, for the coastal bears, the berries are just about done and the grass is dried," Van Tassell said. "The real big pockets of food, the heavy berry concentrations and the fresh green grass are pretty much gone. The bear starts grubbing and becomes an opportunist and stays in cooler, damper places, flipping logs, getting grubs."

"Deer and elk seasons are well underway in October. I've not known black bears to come running to the gun shot the way a brown bear does on Kodiak Island, but if they catch a wind drift with the scent of a gut pile on it,

Bears are most comfortable in forest habitats and some of the best cover is found in the stands of old growth timber left near a two- to five-year-old clearcut. *Photo courtesy Ed Boero*

they'll be following their nose into it."

Over on the dry side, east of the Cascades, the same principle applies.

"I have seen bears active that time of year and they can be just about anywhere where you'll find the deer and elk herds," Van Tassell said. "Don't forget to scout around old orchards for fresh sign. That's the time of year when the apples, pears and plums are falling off the trees and hitting the ground. Rotten or not, the bears will eat it."

This is not a time to squander energy. Oil-rich nuts are a primary food, as are fruits and whatever berries are left. Salmon are also rich in oils. A bear will devour the rotting carcasses in October and November, though he might have ignored them in September when fresh fish were available. Croplands are a target, even harvested crops like corn, where an animal can prospect for leftovers.

In the fall, find the food source. Hunt the water sources too. Not only are the bears bingeing, they're thirstier than usual. October days can be warm and an actively feeding bear will not be far from water. "Look for the north-facing slopes and the timbered draws and for seeps," Van Tassell recommends. Locate a rich food

Follow the Feed

After the rains stop and the green-up begins, bears become more active. Follow the feed, keep your face in the wind and you'll find the bears.

In soggy-side habitat, look for three- to five-year-old isolated clearcuts. Find a clearcut with a creek drainage in it. In the bottom, you'll find plenty of cover. Walk in or use a bicycle to cover ground fast. Bears often use the roads behind locked gates as travel corridors.

Look for tracks along the road and at likely crossing points. Then, step off the road and follow skidder trails and overgrown roads left by long-ago logging operations. Grass, willows, and alders are the first to grow in such places. A bear can find a lot of feed on the new growth. Here, off the beaten path, watch for 'bear tunnels' that lead to swamps and berry patches. Walk quietly, stopping to listen for long periods of time. Bear make a lot of noise when they're on the feed, pulling down brush and nibbling on the tops.

In the first few weeks out of hibernation, bears will focus on new green grass to replenish digestive juices in their stomachs. Just because bears are focused on grass, though, doesn't mean that they won't eat meat. As snows recede and reveal winter-killed deer or elk, the smells wafting with the wind, may bring in a bruin.

source with water and chances are good there'll be a bear nearby.

"I think this is one of the better times of year to try calling because the food sources are more limited and the bears still want to pack on weight. They could very well be more aggressive to the call," Van Tassell said.

UP CLOSE AND PERSONAL When a stalk stalls because the hunter has run out of cover, a call can attract the bear's attention and bring the animal within range. Don't call too loud, a blast of sound is liable to send the bear out of the county. Instead, start soft and make the sound mournful and plaintive, with a continuous wail.

The drawback to a mouth call in this situation is that the bear will pinpoint your position and come in head-on, looking for food and a fight. Be ready to give it to him.

An electronic call, if it can be put into play with a minimum of trouble, can be positioned away from the hunter to allow for a crossing or a broadside shot.

The predator call, a fawn bawl or an injured squirrel, heightens the bear's awareness and raises the stakes.

If there's one thing a hungry bear wants more than anything else, it's an easy meal. And he's used to taking food away from smaller predators. But bears are easily distracted. On the way in, he may stumble across something else he wants to eat. Keep the sound rolling to keep him on the move.

Give him time. Depending on how far he's got to travel, you may see the bruin in a few minutes or an hour. Do your scouting first to make sure there are bears in the area, then keep the wind in your favor and your confidence high. Commit to spending an hour at each call set.

Everything changes when the call is used. The bear may turn aggressive, go passive, be curious or turn tail, depending on his hunger and place in the local bear hierarchy. But calling works often enough that it is a viable option that can bring a bear into bow or handgun range.

Looking for a rug?
Once a bear is spotted, switch to a spotting scope. A good-sized bear will appear to have smaller ears and short legs and walk with a waddle. Conversely, a smaller bear has larger ears in proportion to its head and looks rangy, its legs appearing longer in proportion to its body.
Look at the hide. Bears may rub hair off their front legs, shoulders and flanks. A taxidermist can fix some rubbing, but if your heart is set on a rug, look for a bear with a good pelt.

Late in the fall, the huckleberries and easy living are history. Bears are seeking their food elsewhere. Black bear populations are at all-time highs in southwest Oregon, northeast Oregon and many places in between. In October and early November, they're on the move. The challenge is to think several steps ahead... and get there first.

BLACKTAIL DEER

One hundred grains of Hodgdon Triple 7, a lubed patch, a 320-grain lead conical. With a thump, the ramrod stopped against the seated bullet. The hammer clicked to half cock. I pinched the cap between my teeth and seated it on the nipple.

I reviewed my mental notes. One inch high at 50 yards. Nine inches high at 100. Take a low hold.

The trail led up and out of the creek bottom along a mountainside fringed in oak trees. A half mile in, I leaned the rifle against a fallen tree and began to clack the antlers together to simulate two bucks locking antlers over a doe.

500 yards away, out in the open between the oak trees, a four-point buck stopped and looked back. He was trailing a doe and was not about to go to a fight when he already had a date.

GOLD IN THOSE HILLS

In 1846, Lindsay Applegate, Jesse Applegate and 13 other pioneers established the South Emigrant Trail. From Fort Hall, Idaho, the route headed south following the Humboldt River before passing through the Black Rock Desert in present-day Nevada. The trail then entered northern California and passed Goose and Tule lakes. After crossing the Lost River, the route then crossed the Klamath Basin and the Cascade Range into southern Oregon. The trail then followed Keene Creek to the Siskiyou Mountains where it followed the south branch of the Rogue River. Heading northerly, the wheel ruts followed the Umpqua River before crossing the Calapooyas into the southern Willamette Valley. This route came to be called the Applegate Trail.

Blacktail deer were a staple for the settlers and prospectors that hunted the valleys and on the mountains of southwest Oregon.

For this hunt, I put a Thompson Center 50-caliber Hawken back into service. The gun is styled after the frontier rifle designed by the Hawken brothers of St. Louis, carried in the 1830s, 1840s and 1850s by mountain men, pioneers and prospectors.

Oregon's muzzleloader hunts are restricted by a stringent guideline. A hunter must use open sights and a No. 11 percussion or musket cap and all-lead bullets. Pelletized powder and sabots had not been invented in Lindsay Applegate's day and they are not allowed on an Oregon muzzleloader hunt.

Sighted in at 50 yards, the bullet hits one inch high. At 100 yards, the bullet is nine inches high. Beyond 150, the 320-grain projectile drops like a pumpkin. Like the hunters that first trod these mountains a hundred and sixty years ago, I would have to limit my shots to 100 yards or less.

Rachel Phelps with an Alsea unit blacktail she took in the 2005 season. Phelps times her late-season hunts to coincide with wet weather when more deer are on the move. *Photo courtesy Rachel Phelps*

There was snow in the Cascades when we followed the old route south. It was not hard to imagine a wagon train moving late through the mountains, stopped in some glen banked with snow and the firelight flickering in resolute faces.

My headlights flickered across campground signs and not much else for miles, till the road began to flatten out along the river. The places that make good campsites today were used a hundred and fifty years ago by the people that passed in wagons drawn by oxen.

Fur traders and farmers blazed the trails into the Willamette Valley, but it was prospectors who left their

Lance Manske (left), Gary Lewis and Lee Sandberg with a brace of blacktails and a Columbia whitetail buck.

mark on this valley.

Today, the mines are quiet, but the blacktail deer, upon which many a gold miner fed, are still there.

PROSPECTING FOR A BLACKPOWDER BLACKTAIL
The season was eight days old when we began to prospect for blacktail.

After a look at that buck on the hill the first morning, I met back up with Steve Mathers and we explored a creek drainage along an old mining trail. Down in a canyon, I spotted a doe and then another. A buck followed, but he could only be identified as a buck by the buttons between his ears.

A mature blacktail is bigger through the body than a younger buck or even the oldest doe. Blocky, his neck and shoulders are well-muscled from sparring sessions and battles with other bucks in seasons past.

Most bucks grow to three or four points per side, plus eyeguards, with a rack that tapes between 17 inches and 24 inches wide and tops out at about 15 or 16 inches tall. A few, due to good genetics, minerals in the soil and better nutrition will grow outsize racks that rival trophy mule deer heads.

Furtive by nature, mature bucks seek out places of refuge and pockets that most hunters pass up. Bucks stake out a small home range, often in the company of one or two others, fattening up in late summer and early fall. When hunters take to the woods in September and October, many bucks change their patterns, moving at night to feed and water. It is only in the cool of November, when the rains fall and the rut comes on, that they let their guard down a little and a hunter can find more weaknesses in a big buck's defense; chinks in his armor.

BEATING A BLACKTAIL'S DEFENSES
From the time the velvet is shed, bucks use their antlers to spar. The clash and click of bone can bring other deer in for a look. The behavior intensifies as the rut looms. Tickling the tines and grunting can bring a buck to investigate at any time of the year, but it is most likely to happen late in October and early November, when a dominant buck may come in to drive away younger interlopers.

Appeal to aggression to bring them in, or make a plea for motherly intervention.

Early in the season, a varmint call is of little use, save to put deer on alert. In November, when bucks are following does, a fawn-in-distress call can draw in a protective doe that might be trailed by a buck. A high percentage of does lose their fawns to predators each spring and summer. The plaintive sounds of a fawn going under the sharp teeth of a pack of coyotes is not soon forgotten. Does often come to the call. In the breeding season there is a good chance they have a buck hot on their heels, because of the enticing scent of the female in the breeding season.

The best thing a hunter can do to get within muzzleloader range is to use the breeze to their advantage. For most of us, most of the time, that means the wind in the face, and an approach from downwind. Tie a thread or a feather to the gun barrel, or use Smoke-In-A-Bottle or a similar product to divine the vagaries of the breeze.

The Stalk
When the sun was low in the west, I ghosted up a hill on a northwest slope. The ground was damp, but I found a dry

Blacktail sanctuaries provide both food and cover. When pressured, bucks pull back to these core areas.

deer bed. Standing there, I turned and looked down the hill and could see the Jeep through the trees. There were several other beds above the first. Each afforded a strategic view of

Poison Oak
By Gary Burris

There's likely nothing in the Oregon landscape that causes hunters more grief and misery than poison oak. For those who've had the irritating rash it's the incessant itching, burning and weeping that can make a hunter contemplate giving up hunting all together.

Most of the United States battles poison ivy while Oregon hunters go toe to toe with poison oak. Although there are slight variations in the look of the plants, the ways in which poison oak or ivy can ravage a person's body are identical.

So, what is the one thing every person should know about poison oak and ivy? Urushiol. Once a person understands exactly what urushiol (say "oo-roo-she-all") is, and how long lasting and potent the substance can be, preventing or stopping the rash from spreading becomes a lot less difficult.

Urushiol is an invisible, resin-like substance that is found in nearly every fiber of poison oak and ivy plants. It locks on to proteins in the skin within 20 minutes to form a seemingly unshakeable bond. Even the slightest amount of urushiol on a person's skin can cause a human body to explode into a nasty rash within 24 to 48 hours. Urushiol will remain toxic for years and is so potent that the amount that could fit on the tip of a needle is enough to trigger a reaction in hundreds of people. Regular soap and water will not remove urushiol after it has bound to skin, it will only spread the urushiol around.

The great news is that there are products on the market to remove urushiol. An Oregon company, Tec Labs, makes an excellent product called Tecnu Extreme Medicated Poison Ivy Scrub. It's available at all major drug store chains in the U.S., plus Oregon favorites like Bi-Mart, Fred Meyer and Ray's Markets. It's the first all-in-one product to help prevent a rash or stop an existing rash from spreading.

Tecnu Extreme can be used at any point to help prevent a rash after exposure, but prior to the rash appearing; however, the sooner the better. If a rash starts to break out, a person should immediately do an all over application to help stop the rash in its tracks and start the healing process.

---

the road or approaches that would bring a hunter or a cat or a coyote into striking distance.

Those deer must have sounded the alarm, because, in the stand of oaks at the knife-edge top of the ridge, where I should have spotted at least a couple of does, nothing moved. Nothing save the branches that whispered in the breeze off the Siskiyous.

A deer trail led me down through the poison oak and I crossed the road in the failing light.

I skirted the top of a canyon and picked up another deer trail. For some minutes I listened and began to imagine a deer moving in the leaves below. With binoculars up, I scanned the oaks and firs down slope. There – a barrel-shaped horizontal against vertical tree trunks. The binocular resolved an ear, an antler.

The next morning, my friend John McDevitt was along. The sun was high in the sky when McDevitt spotted a buck in the canyon. We were less than a quarter mile from where I had seen the buck the night before. I had taken the cap from under the hammer, but it was a matter of a moment to pinch it back on. One pass with the binocular was enough. I eased the hammer back and muffled the click to full cock with the blade of the trigger.

Distracted by a hot doe, the buck had let his defenses down. No time for the rangefinder. Eighty yards, not more than a hundred. Steep. 'Nine inches high at 100. Hold low,' I told myself. 'Even lower for this steep downhill shot.'

He stopped. I put the front post beneath the deer and stroked the trigger. The Hawken rocked me with the recoil and a cloud of white smoke hung in the still air. The doe jumped a log, made another bound and disappeared into the trees. The buck lay stretched out, dropped by the bullet that struck it high through the top of the lungs.

Out of habit, I loaded again from my possibles bag. 100

grains of powder, a patch, the bullet seated home, a crimped cap on the nipple.

With a bearing on where the deer lay, we walked down through the trees, through golden shafts of sunlight beaming through the branches. Gray around the muzzle, the buck was muscular, summer-fat with tall nut-brown antlers, almost 17 inches wide. Three points on one side and four on the other. There was work to do.

HOME RANGE AND HABITAT Due in part to their narrow geographic range, blacktailed deer are largely ignored in the popular hunting press, but this animal is one of America's most prized trophies. Blacktails are a subspecies of mule deer and their territories overlap along the eastern boundaries of the smaller deer's range. A blacktail doe weighs 70 to 140 pounds. Bucks weigh between 120 and 250 pounds. A buck may measure up to 36 inches at the shoulder.

They are called blacktails because the bottom two-thirds of the tail is black. The tail is wider than a mule deer's tail. At the base, it is brown. The underside is white. Blacktail deer are reddish-brown in the summer and tend to go grey-brown in the fall.

Dave Pitts picked up the muzzleloader after he read the family diary and found an account of an 1857 whitetail hunt.

If you want to see blacktails, watch clearcuts and burns. Logging opens up the forest canopy to let in the sunshine. New growth springs up and deer can find most of what they need all in one place.

Deer need food, water, shelter, and space. Sometimes they get all four in a clearcut. They also become vulnerable to hunters. That's why you will only find does, fawns, and immature bucks in large openings.

If you want to fill your tag with a doe (when legal) or a young buck, hunt the clearcuts in the morning, bedding areas at noon, and paths leading from bedding areas in late afternoon. You will find the deer.

Think Small to Find Un-Pressured Bucks

If your scouting paid off with a glimpse of a big buck's track, don't assume that he left the county when the sun came up on opening day. Likely, he's still there spending the daylight hours under cover.

It doesn't take much habitat to hide a deer and many big blacktail bucks grow old without ever being seen by a hunter. Their sanctuaries provide both cover and food. Water can be reached after dark. During the general rifle season, bucks may spend most of their time in an area of just a few acres.

To find such an animal, think small. A strip of trees between roads can hold a deer. A half-acre behind the barn may hold a buck. As will an island in a river or a lake. You may find such a spot anywhere in blacktail country.

A buck living in such a sanctuary may not get as much pressure as most public land bucks. Set up a one-man drive with a stander at the back door or still-hunt solo with the wind in your face. Go slow and don't overlook even the smallest cover. Focus on the goal, stay out all day, and hunt into the wind.

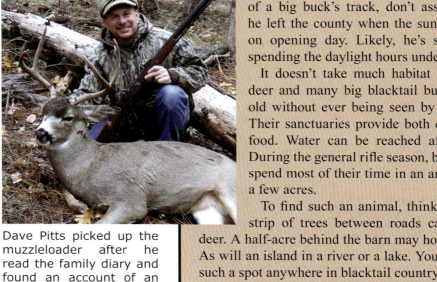

However, clearcuts are not as easy to find as they once were. Now, chemicals are used to control weeds, what we hunters refer to as forbs and what deer call groceries.

Blacktail deer are among the most wary of big game animals. Learn their habits, their preferred foods and bedding areas. Scouting pays off with more deer sightings during the season.

Today's super-fast growing tree seedlings turn clearcuts into tall timber again a lot faster than they used to.

Also, fear of fire may keep gates closed to timber company lands in low-water years, with "No Access" signs posted until the rains come. As blacktails adapt, so do hunters.

TACTICS FOR TODAY'S BLACKTAIL HUNTER

For a crack at a big buck, look at what the orange-clad horde is doing and do the opposite. Many hunters know only the old way of hunting: park in a landing and watch the hillside; or hope that a buck dashes across the road.

A better strategy is to look for the pockets the crowds pass by. Sometimes they may be so obvious that no one would think to hunt there. Sometimes they are so far back in the timber or the brush is so thick that other hunters detour around it.

In oak savannah, the hills are often bare, especially the south-facing exposures. Blackberry bushes, poison oak, oak trees and scattered pines grow up the sides, with bedding cover found in the run-off washes and along the creek bottoms. Old road beds provide dependable travel corridors and trails are visible from hundreds of yards away, showing where a hunter might expect to see a deer emerge from the heavy cover.

Deer are easily seen from the tops of the hills, but usually, glimpses of does and forked horns are the pay-off. Wiser bucks know to bed in the sticker patches when hunters take to the ridges. The bigger bucks have seen it all before.

FINDING DEER IN POCKETS OF COVER To find pockets that other people pass by, use a 7.5 Minute Series, 1:24000 U.S. Geological Survey map. With the contour intervals of 40 feet on a 7.5 minute topo, it's easy to pinpoint roadless areas, identify swamps, spot north-facing ridges and locate most of the springs and seeps. A hunter can also identify escape routes and make an estimate at where to find the dense cover where deer bed.

In these hideouts, most big blacktail bucks grow old without ever being seen by a hunter. Their sanctuaries provide both cover and food. Water can be reached after dark. During the general rifle season, bucks spend most of their time in an area of just a few acres and feed after the sun goes down.

Private land may be the key to access, even to public ground. Get permission to cross a neighbor's land. If parking pull-outs are few and far between, have someone drop you off along the road. If a stream is the boundary, use waders or float a boat. Whatever it takes, hunt the ground other hunters can't or won't get to. And don't fall into their patterns.

When scouting for blacktails, look for the pockets that the crowds pass by. Old road beds provide dependable travel corridors and trails may be visible from hundreds of yards away where a hunter might expect to see a deer emerge from heavy cover.

Mature blacktails seldom come easy. Examine aerial photos and topo maps to find the places where the big boys live. Locate natural escape routes such as saddles and canyons. Look for brushy shelves where a buck can watch

Youth hunts and antlerless seasons offer youngsters a chance to experience the hunt with a higher likelihood of success. Such hunts are used as management tools by ODFW.

his backtrail from his bed. Locate a trail from a nearby feeding area or water and you have found a buck's living room.

Hunt into the wind and watch every step. Move too fast and deer will see you before you spot them. Slow down. Every time you take a step, a new window opens in the heavy cover. Look for the horizontal line of a back, the black of a nose, the flick of a tail, the crook of a leg, or sunlight glinting from nut-brown antler. Carry binoculars on a harness against your chest, not in a daypack. And use them.

Bring your lunch and stay in the woods all day. Watch a trail leading into a bedding area and let other hunters push the deer your way.

In the timber, hunt from above, whether from a tree stand or looking down from a high cliff. Such stands afford greater visibility, keep you above the line of sight, and keep your scent stream above the game.

In open country, use a spotting scope to scout bucks on distant hilltops. It's always better to see them first and plan a strategy.

This three-point blacktail was bedded in the blackberry bushes, with two other deer as sentries.

MULE DEER

The third day of the season was the warmest yet. We hiked onto the mountain where I had taken a good buck the season before, but water was scarce and fresh deer tracks were even scarcer. There were more tracks down lower, close to water and ranchlands. Still, we hunted, looking into draws, and scanning beneath the rim for holed-up mule deer. A big buck was our goal and we didn't expect to find him in the lowlands.

Once we heard coyotes, close by, running down a deer, unseen for the thick juniper trees on the ridge.

As morning gave way to afternoon, we changed tactics, and hunted the bedding areas on the slopes of the mountain. Nothing. We hunted downhill and looked over the edge of the canyon into likely bedding spots. Nothing.

There is a point in a hunt when intensity lets off like a pressure relief valve. We hit that spot at about 1:30 in the afternoon. Even as we let our guard down and began to joke and whisper, we kept watch. At times like this we have come on deer in their beds and blown our opportunities.

A John Day River country mule deer in his summer coat.

We would have walked right by those deer if it hadn't been for that cagey old buck getting nervous. He hooked a doe in the backside and she leaped away.

I saw gray flashing through the junipers and pulled up my binoculars. A doe. Then a second and third, making their escape. James had his rifle up, ready. No antlers.

Still we watched, waiting. Too often we had been surprised by the sudden appearance of a doe or young buck, then missed the opportunity at a larger buck when our guard was down.

There. The buck headed in the opposite direction the does had taken. James swung his rifle to his shoulder as the deer bounded straight away. He fired and missed, the deer vanishing in the junipers, leaving me with no shot. We followed.

As we had done for three days now, we went into two-man drive mode, walking forty yards apart, parallel to each other through the junipers along the rim.

The sun beat down and there was little shade. We followed the buck as he made his way up and down through washes and around rocky outcroppings. Catching glimpses of gray-brown hair and golden antler through the green junipers and silver sage, we

BIG GAME - MULE DEER

These two mule deer bucks were feeding with the does, high on the mountain in the afternoon of opening day. A long stalk put the hunters in range.

followed.

He turned a hard left and came out into the sunlight, running. I threw my rifle to my shoulder, swinging the crosshairs across his body. Leading him in the brief opening in the trees, I snicked off the safety and squeezed the trigger.

The 160-grain Nosler Partition threw that buck for a loop, slamming him to the ground.

After the shot, I shook with the adrenaline that coursed through my body. I could see from this far away that I had killed a big buck. Pacing off the distance allowed me to calm my nerves. I counted 137 yards. Then came the slaps on the back for this end to a hard hunt. We admired the antlers and the fine shiny coat and breathed in the familiar smell of these bucks of the sage.

The buck was heavy and his antlers taped 28-1/2 inches wide, with four points per side and hooked eye guards.

It took two hours to cape, skin and quarter, then another two hours to pack it a mile and a half out to the road.

We found a spring burbling water into a cattle tank. This was why the deer weren't bedded up high as they usually are at this time of year. With little rain in the past few months, other sources had dried up. My buck had bedded in the forest rather than on the mountain to be closer to water. Something to keep in mind. And I won't forget how a two-man drive can allow one hunter to push a big buck to another hunter working parallel.

We cupped hands to catch the water, letting it run down, cool and refreshing, over our heads as the moon came up over the mountain.

The mule deer, with its out-sized ears, is the largest of the three main species of North American deer. Its hooves are larger and blunter than those of other deer, allowing them to negotiate snow and rugged ground. It is a creature aptly suited to the harsh existence of life in the high desert.

Though mule deer are a common sight in eastern Oregon, the mature adult buck is a secretive, adaptive animal that makes its living largely unseen in a rugged land.

PLANNING THE HUNT

Today's mule deer hunter is a long-range planner. To draw a hunt in some eastern Oregon units takes ten years or more of application, of crossing one's fingers and praying for a tag. To make matters worse, conditions may improve or decline over the years. If the hunter is not paying attention, he may draw a coveted tag in a unit with lower deer numbers than when he started applying years before. It pays to know what factors

A gorgeous buck from the juniper country. *Photo courtesy Bill Truxal*

are at work in the habitat.

In the off seasons, when the June 20 postcard reads UNSUCCESSFUL FOR BUCK DEER, the best hunters go scouting anyway, or serve as camp help for their friends who were lucky in the tag lottery. And year-round, coyote and cougar hunts go a long way toward helping a hunter learn a prospective unit and they have the added benefit of keeping predator numbers in check.

The Oregon Big Game Regulations book is the place to start when planning a hunt. After that, one of the best resources is the Oregon Tag Guide, which shows the likelihood of drawing a tag and the last three years of harvest statistics.

The Record Book of Oregon's Big Game Animals (www.nwbiggame.com) provides clues as to which counties produce the most and biggest heads.

Biologists are a wealth of information, but most people don't tap in to this resource funded by their license and tag fees. Contact phone numbers and email addresses are available on the Oregon Department of Fish and Wildlife web site at www.dfw.state.or.us.

Daily movements usually begin with mule deer moving to feeding areas like a grassy margin. They feed until one to two hours after sunrise then bed nearby.

Oregon has more public land than most states and much of it can be found in the dry, southeastern corner, made up of the Wagontire, Juniper, Malheur River, Beulah, Owyhee, Whitehorse, Steens Mountain, Beatys Butte, Warner and Interstate units.

Of these, the Beulah (57%), Interstate (58%) and Warner (60%) units have the least public land. The Whitehorse (91%), Juniper (90%) and Beatys Butte (89%) have the best access.

The units managed for hunter opportunity have higher tag numbers (more hunters), while the trophy units are harder to draw.

BACKCOUNTRY HUNTING The travel companies and chambers of commerce call this southeastern corner of the state Oregon's Outback. Yes, it is spectacular. There is no other country like it. The community of Burns and Hines, located where the corners of the Silvies, Malheur River, Juniper and Steens Mountains units come together, is the commercial hub of southeast Oregon. Roads extend away from Burns/Hines like spokes from a wheel.

After the first five days of rifle season, when everyone else has headed for home, a hunter can traverse miles of desert without seeing another human. Grocery stores and restaurants in communities like Juntura, Jordan Valley, Paisley, Bly and Bonanza keep uncertain hours. Fuel stations are few and far between, so the veteran of southeast Oregon fills up at every station and carries an extra five or ten gallons in safety cans.

What the first time visitor might remember more than anything else are the roads. They will turn a two-wheel drive pickup meant for city driving into a rattling bucket of bolts in just a few miles. Only four-wheel drive rigs with high clearance need apply. And bring not one spare tire, but two spares and tire chains because the character of the roads change when it rains. All that dust that blows in the rearview mirror turns to gumbo overnight.

There are snakes. The best way to handle snakes is to never encounter them in the first place. One eastern Oregon guide I know throws stones ahead

of him, to warn the rattlers that he's coming. Similarly, a person can carry a staff and rap it on the ground, sending vibrations that the snakes can sense, allowing them time to move away. Rattlesnakes buzz to warn you of their presence. Usually they'll only strike when threatened so give them time to get away

Carry a snake bite kit. If you, or a member of your party, are bitten, then seek help immediately. Your trip is over. Don't let the victim overexert on the way back, it only spreads the poison faster.

Speaking of poison, don't forget the scorpions. Hunting spiders and other insects at night, scorpions retreat to cool shadows in the daytime. I found them beneath flat rocks while on a hunt in the Malheur River country. Their bite will probably ruin your day and could possibly be fatal. Out looking for food at night, they could end up in your tent by morning. It pays to be careful.

Shake your boots out before stepping in. A spider may have sought refuge from the scorpions there. Most spider bites are harmless but the black widow, a large spider with a black body and red hourglass on the abdomen, is venomous. Their bite is painful though seldom fatal, a particle

After a fire, new growth pushes up through the ashes. Such places bring in the game to feed on the tender shoots. *Photo courtesy Battle Creek Outfitters*

A young mule deer in velvet. On summer scouting trips, look for deer out in the open. At this time of year, bucks spend their days in open spaces to protect the developing antlers.

of knowledge that might be comforting sometime.

Don't think I'm trying to keep you out of the desert. I wouldn't want to be accused of trying to scare you. It's not like I mentioned ground squirrels with fleas that carry bubonic plague, wasps, fever-carrying deer ticks, bats or rabid skunks, though I could have.

Just be careful when you hike the canyon trails or glass a buck from some stony outcrop. Sometime toward mid-afternoon, you might stop what you're doing and look to the sky. There might be vultures circling above the rim or watching from some rocky ledge. They are up there for a reason.

MULEY SUBTERFUGE Where water holes are scarce, it isn't hard to find deer sign, if you know where to look. Spend a day scouting near water and you'll find evidence aplenty. Once you locate a buck's track, stop and look around. Chances are he's no more than a half-mile away. We know this, but mule deer remain a mystery. Especially the big bucks that run with the herd and the outsized loners that use every trick in

the book to keep from being seen.

In eastern Oregon, mule deer bucks can vanish – using cunning and trickery instead of speed and distance to stay out of sight. At the first hint of trouble, they go into crisis management mode.

Bucks use other deer as scouts to alert them to trails with them until he senses danger. At the first opportunity, he lets the females go and uses cover or distance to throw a hunter off his track. While the hunter watches the does, the buck makes his getaway.

THE SCOUTING TRIP With your binoculars and spotting scope, now is the time to plan your approach for the coming hunt. If you are hunting in the wide-open of Lake, Malheur or Harney counties, you can use spot-and-stalk tactics. If there will be enough people in your party, you might employ a drive, or sit on a saddle to intercept deer moving from one drainage to another. Think low-impact.

Mule deer hunting in open country lends itself to the spot-and-stalk method. Get to the highest part of your hunting area before shooting light.

A mule deer's survival strategy includes identifying the predator then putting distance and obstacles between himself and danger.

danger, or as decoys to draw the attention of predators. When danger nears, the buck will drive out his buddy on the tips of his antlers, hoping to draw the eye of the hunter, while he, belly on the ground, sneaks away in the other direction or lays his antlers in the sage.

Another favorite tactic involves using a herd of does. When the season opener finds a buck in the proximity of a herd of two or more does, the veteran

Approach the target area from out of sight. Don't cross openings. Move from cover to cover, as if you were carrying a rifle instead of glasses. Set up your spotting scope in the shade of a tree where you have good visibility, then wait and watch. Resist the urge to start walking trails, unless you want to lower your odds of success.

You may want to hunt from a perch in a tree or set up a ground blind. If your plan calls for the use of a stand, you have no choice but to walk the trails to find

The chances of spotting muleys in the open are best in the morning, and evening.

a place to put it. Pre-trip planning with maps and aerial photos is even more important, so you can minimize impact.

The scouting trip is also the time to pick a campsite. Pick several alternates in case someone beats you to your first choice. Don't camp where the deer will hear you pound tent stakes, or smell last year's venison on the grill. They've been through this before. The more warning you give, the better the chance they'll keep you from notching your tag this year.

Keep alternate plans. You need a fall-back position in case other hunters beat you to your spot, or camp where you planned to hunt.

Darren Roe (pictured below) arrowed this big Klamath Basin buck at 12 yards after a long stalk. *Photo courtesy Roe Outfitters*

The Pious Report (1989) found that a mule deer's diet consists of 55% browse (the new growth of trees, shrubs and vines), 22% forbs (broadleaf plants), 10% grasses, 7% nuts and 6% other materials. *Photo courtesy John Milton*

SPOT AND STALK FOR MULE DEER

Rough, broken country makes good mule deer habitat. When the weather is warm, look for deer beds on cool, north-facing slopes. But in order to find animals, locate the food then locate the water.

Stand-hunt along corridors between feeding and bedding areas. Conceal yourself behind a natural feature like a rock outcrop or large tree, or use a tree stand.

The Pious Report (1989) found that a mule deer's diet consists of 55% browse (the new growth of trees, shrubs and vines), 22% forbs (broadleaf plants), 10% grasses, 7% nuts and 6% other materials. The best bet is to focus on food sources like bitterbrush and mountain mahogany.

Plant the tripod in the moon-shadow of a juniper, then put an eye to the spotting scope with the first rays of the sun. It may take an hour or more to spot the first deer. Look for parts: the horizontal line of the back, the crook of a back leg, the white of a rump or the glint of sun on antler. Then watch as the buck searches out a bed by mid-morning.

A buck will seek a resting place from which he can see in many directions or a hole in the thick stuff where anybody approaching will make a lot of noise. If it is warm, he'll make his bed in the shade. There will always be an escape route.

And more often than not, he'll use it before the stalk brings a hunter within rifle range. But that's the challenge of the hunt out on the dry side.

We will walk those canyons and top out the ridges and drink in the rarefied high desert air. If fortune

Big mule deer bucks often bed in the sagebrush, sometimes alone, but more often with a younger buck or does to use as decoys.

smiles and the deer we see have antlers, we will pack our winter's meat back down. If the deer are quick and our reactions are slow, we count it reward enough that we were there.

WHITETAIL DEER (EASTERN OR)

Football Season's Biggest Game

Every year, thousands of parents and their offspring are forced to make a decision between two great passions of autumn: football and hunting. This year, 12 year-old Jacob Lum, a wide receiver on his middle school football team, had to decide what was most important to him. Fortunately, his football coaches understood.

"Lum," his coach said, "it better be a big one."

The buck he was after was certainly a big one. While scouting for deer, Jacob and his father Tod had hunted bear and grouse in the Snake and Imnaha units the previous month. The pair spotted a big whitetail they thought they might be able to find again.

From where the Lums live in Roseburg, their destination in northeast Oregon was 500 miles away. With gas prices averaging $2.95 a gallon, it was not an easy decision to load up the truck and head east for a two-day hunt.

On Thursday night at 9pm, the hunters started on the 12-hour drive and stopped to sleep in the Cascades. Friday morning, after breakfast, they started east again, watching antelope, geese, ducks, quail and herds of deer. Jacob worked on homework most of the way. As light was fading from the evening sky, the hunters arrived at camp. There were deer on the hills and dark clouds in the sky. The weather forecast called for a 60 percent chance of showers.

With the morning came the rain. The alarm rang at 4:30am. By 5:30, with the hint of sunlight on the eastern horizon, the hunters started up the hill. It was too early to start. A doe let them know about it as they spooked her. She bolted uphill, spooking the rest of the herd. The Lums waited and watched as the sun pushed back the night.

Now the deer were wary. Stiff-legged, the animals walked out of the grassy bottoms and bedded high on the hill up against the hawthorn berries. From their perch, they watched the fields and valley below.

Tod began to strategize. "Our plan was to circle around and sneak up on them, hoping to get a chance at the big buck in the group." The only problem was that there was no cover. Tod, who grew up bowhunting the spooky axis deer and Spanish goats in Hawaii, knew they'd have to improvise.

"Grab my belt," he told Jacob, "and bend your head down. We'll pretend we're a four-legged animal." It worked. The deer watched, curious, but did not spook. Finally, the Lums reached a bench that gave them the cover to move out of sight, into a stand of trees along a fence line. A small forked horn buck with only one antler stood watching. A legal buck, only 60 yards away. Tod waited to see what his boy would do.

Jacob remembered the words of his coach. "It better be a big one." A one-antlered forked horn wasn't the buck he was looking for. Somewhere on the other side of the hill, there was a big buck.

Now in the thicker cover of the hawthorn bushes, Tod and Jacob closed in on the last known position of the buck

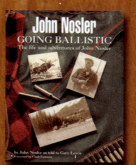

When hunters want bullets they can depend on, the name they trust, more than any other, is Nosler.

You know his bullets, now read his story.

For a signed copy of the hardcover *John Nosler Going Ballistic*, send $29.95 to Gary Lewis Outdoors PO Box 1364 Bend, OR 97709 or visit

www.GaryLewisOutdoors.com

With his eye on the goal, 12 year-old Jacob Lum passed up a smaller forked horn for a chance at this great northeastern Oregon whitetail. *Photo courtesy Tod Lum*

and does they had spooked earlier in the morning. But the deer had moved. Now they fed out in the open. The nearest animals were 150 yards away.

Jacob gulped the clean mountain air in large gasps. "I'm not tired," he told his dad, "just too excited." The hawthorn bushes allowed them to get a little closer and they crawled on hands and knees through the tall, wet grass.

Finally, Tod whispered to Jacob, "This is it, you can make this shot. Just relax, rest your rifle on my backpack and remember what we practiced - breathing, squeezing. You can do this."

There was water on the scope and Tod wiped the lenses. Jacob said he could see. There were five deer. Now they had resumed feeding and looked around from time to time, probably hoping for a second look at the goofy four-legger they'd seen down the slope earlier in the morning.

Jacob lay down prone in the grass and squared up with the buck. To Tod, it seemed like forever as he watched the buck in his fogged binoculars.

This was the moment of truth. Jacob had passed up an easy shot at a forked horn for a chance to take this buck. Would the work and the scouting and the hours spent in practice pay off?

Jacob's 260 Ruger M77 rifle was fed with a handloaded 140-grain Nosler Partition on 38 grains of IMR 4350. The 12 year-old had practiced throughout the spring and summer in anticipation of this moment.

Jacob eased the rifle's safety off, snugged the butt into his shoulder, welded his cheek to the stock, steadied the crosshair and took the slack out of the trigger.

The rifle cracked and the buck reared up on his hind legs, lurched forward and ran 50 yards over the crest of the hill and out of sight.

Jacob bolted another round into the chamber and the hunters followed. They found the buck on the other side of hill.

The 140-grain Nosler Partition bullet had completely passed through both lungs and did its job. The preparation, the 12-hour drive and Jacob's focus had paid off with an extraordinary whitetail buck.

To get to the point where Jacob could wrap his hands around the antlers and count the points, the young man learned that preparation and anticipation are as important as the hunt. Passion pushed him when it was easier to stay home, go to football practice and do homework. And the skills he learned in a summer of training paid off in the thrill of his first deer hunt. Like his football coaches knew, the focus and the work that the 12 year-old put into his first big game season will serve him well wherever his future takes him.

Associated with stream bottoms and agricultural edges, the whitetail deer that make their living in northeast Oregon are found in highest numbers in Wallowa, Baker, Umatilla, and Union counties. Whitetails may also be found living alongside mule deer in Morrow, Grant and Wasco counties.

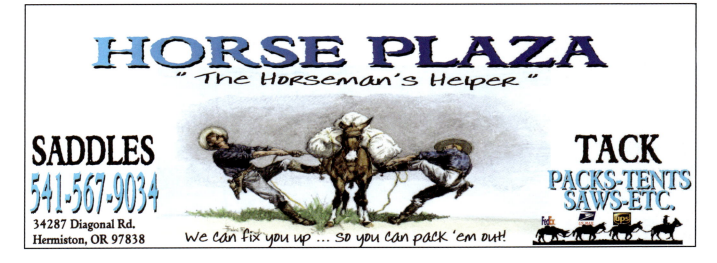

COLUMBIA WHITETAIL DEER

Lewis and Clark's Whitetail

My guide wore a confident smile. We sat parked at a steel gate leading into a 500-acre parcel of rolling ranchland. "Normally I wouldn't think about hunting this little pocket first, but I saw a big buck here about this time yesterday and we're going to make a play for him."

A week ago, the rolling oak savannah had been burned and now the hills were in green-up. We expected to see deer out on the hillsides, nibbling at the new shoots in the afternoon sunlight.

For the first time in almost 30 years, the state of Oregon held a hunt for the little-known Columbian whitetail. There were a limited number of tags, but one of them had my name on it.

On foot, we eased up the road that followed the creek bottom. "We're looking for a specific buck," Lance whispered. "We've found him twice in the last two weeks. He's probably 20 inches wide with the longest eyeguards I've ever seen. We're going to see some others, but he's the one we're after."

The valley opened in front of us and a west breeze blew in our faces. Blackberries grew through the axles of a broken-down tractor and over the porch of the house. Three does were bedded in the shade. They stood as we approached, then danced off, their long white tails waving in flight.

A Columbia whitetail buck in the fog.

An Uncommon Whitetail

Meriwether Lewis, familiar with the whitetail deer in his home state of Virginia, was the first to describe western mule deer and blacktails for science. And on February 19, 1806, the Lewis & Clark journals record the following about an uncommon whitetail the expedition called "the common red deer."

"The common red deer we found under the Rocky Mountains in the neighborhood of the Chopunnish, and about the great falls of the Columbia River and as low down the same as the commencement of tide water. These do not appear to differ essentially from those of our country being about the same size, shape and appearance in every respect except their great

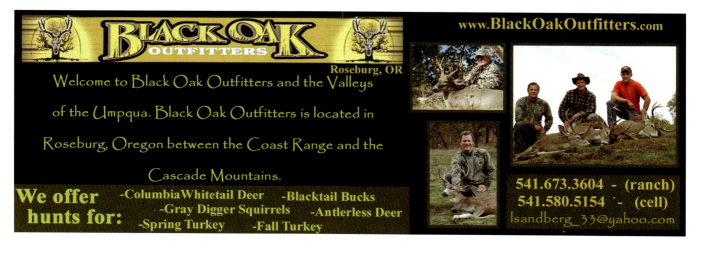

length of tail which is more than half as long again as our deer. I measured one of them, which was 17 inches long."

Now that's an uncommonly long tail, longer than you're likely to find on any whitetail, but today, this 'common red deer' is recognized as the westernmost variety of 38 subspecies of whitetail. The Columbian whitetail. And this season (2005), for the first time in almost 30 years, Oregon hunters had a chance to hunt them.

The 'common red deer' became less common in the early 1900s as poachers took their toll and farmland displaced habitat. In the 1930s some feared the deer was extinct, but remnant populations were found. In the late 1960s, biologists estimated there were less than 1000 animals left. In the 1970s, the Columbian whitetail was listed under the Federal Endangered Species Act and the recovery effort was underway.

Today, two distinct groups remain; a thriving population of about 6,200 animals in Douglas County, and approximately 800 deer in the Columbia drainage, inhabiting several islands and the mainland on both shores.

The Columbian whitetail was de-listed in 2003 when management of the herd was turned back over from the Federal government to the Oregon Department of Fish and Wildlife. The first season in almost 30 years was held in 2005. Twenty-three tags were made available to the public and 110 tags were issued to private landowners in the region through the Department's Land Owner Preference tag program.

I chose Roseburg-based Black Oak Outfitters. Partners Lance Manske and George Sandberg lease hunting rights on several ranches in the Dixonville area, east of Roseburg. I hunted with Lance and a filmmaker from Wolf Creek Productions, Ryan Cornish.

Sneaking and Peeking

Every fold of ground opened new views into the habitat. On the far slope we counted over 20 deer, in twos and threes, feeding in the late afternoon light. One buck fed out into the open from a clump of blackberries, then disappeared in the shade of a black oak. Two more bucks fed together on a flat halfway up the slope. Lance said we'd make a stalk on one if we failed to find the buck we were after. "He was on this hill, beyond those thistles on the edge of that little valley. We'll find him."

Wild turkeys – two flocks of jakes and long-bearded toms – fed on the slope above us. One went into full strut and the other birds bullied him back down the hill. Across the canyon a small whitetail doe fed out of a streambed. 200 yards away, a doe and her twins nibbled blackberries along an old two-track. Now our light was failing fast. In 45 minutes or less the sun would be gone. We moved faster, checking each drainage as we reached it.

Ryan put down his camera and peered through his binoculars. "There. In the corner of that field. A buck coming down the fence line."

Lance stopped and picked up his glasses. He was silent for a moment. "That's the buck we want," he said. "And on this side of the fence is another that might be just as good. They're probably 600 yards out."

We started down the hill, staying in the lengthening shadows of the oaks. If we took too long getting into position, we'd lose our light and our chance.

Near the bottom of the valley, we paused and checked our quarry with the binoculars. The bucks had bedded, one on our side of the fence and one on the other.

I flopped down on my belly beneath an oak tree and rested the rifle on my fanny pack. Lance was seated behind and to my right. With his rangefinder, he shot the tree behind the deer. Three hundred yards. That meant the buck was at 298. I dialed my scope to 8-power and snicked the safety to 'fire'.

My ears pounded with my pulse. I had to be careful not to transmit that energy to the trigger. There, the crosshairs were steady, the trigger broke and the scope filled with an orange bloom.

I rocked with the recoil, and bolted another round in the chamber. The buck lay still, while the other buck stood,

Columbia whitetails and blacktails can share the same habitat. Learn to look at distinguishing features. A long tail fringed in white, distinct rings around eyes and ears and antlers with tines from the main beam, are hallmarks of a whitetail.

his head held high. He ran a few yards then stopped to look back. In another moment, he'd disappeared. We started down the hill and across the canyon.

There on that slope, with the sun going down, I put my hand on my first Columbian whitetail. A stalk I'll never forget and the buck of a lifetime.

He had a broad white tail (it measured ten inches long), a sleek brown coat and white circles around his eyes. His teeth were worn and he had antlers that measured almost 20 inches wide with six-inch eyeguards. A buck we in the West would call a three-point and what easterners would call an eight-pointer. I guessed he'd tip the scales at 150 pounds.

Since that 2005 hunt, the opportunity has been expanded to include a hunt in the North Bank Habitat Management Area, a public reserve near the town of Roseburg. It has been a long time since hunters have pursued this interesting subspecies of whitetail. Thanks to scientific management and the patience of landowners in the Umpqua Valley, Lewis and Clark's 'common red deer,' the uncommon Columbian whitetail is back. ■

PRONGHORN ANTELOPE

"The ground rose in a gentle swell, crested at a low ridge, troughed in a grassy valley and crested again, tipped with low sagebrush at the top like a breaking wave. The pronghorn buck looked to be at least 1200 yards away.

Jerry, who had tagged his antelope on the first day of the season, said "This looks like a job for ol' Bossy."

If ever there was a time to employ the moovable blind, it was now. Jerry had built the Black Angus impostor out of stiff cardboard with plywood backing and a wooden handle. With a razor blade, he crafted a bovine noggin that would have fit in at any feedlot.

To a pronghorn antelope in Oregon's Malheur River unit, there must be no more familiar profile. Spray-painted black, it looked like 90 percent of the beef in our western desert.

Jerry hid the truck behind a rise and we started out through the sagebrush with the cardboard cow lifted high. After we'd covered 300 yards, we stopped, lowering ol' Bossy to the ground while we knelt behind her. I noticed that my rifle barrel glinted in the sunlight, so I moved it to the shadow in my left hand.

With his hands cupped, Jerry moo-ed like a lost heifer. I leaned beneath the bovine head and took a look. Now I could see two bucks. The smaller buck stood alone on our right. The buck we were after stood on the left, his does behind him.

So far it was working. We fooled a jackrabbit that let us approach to less than ten feet, then turned nearly inside out when he realized he'd been tricked.

For 200 yards we were concealed by the low ridge. We made good time to the top then slipped over the other side. We had their attention. Then we felt the wind change direction.

For some time, our cow had been walking sideways. The antelope got used to that. Now our bovine would walk backwards to stay downwind. 500 yards now. For the first time, I got a good look at the herd buck. He carried horns that were wide and at least twice the length of his ears.

We zigged and zagged and bawled and rested, moo-ving ever closer. I waited until we were less than 300 yards away

Gary Lewis demonstrates the use of the bogus bovine. 'Bossy' helped the hunters get within range of a big buck.

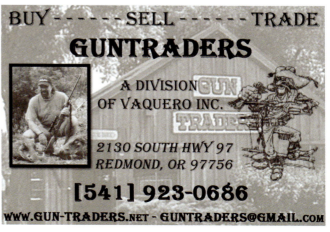

before I put my hand on Jerry's shoulder and stopped him.

Jerry lowered the cow and I peered under Bossy's head, ready to go prone and make my shot.

They were gone. The big backwards bovine with long legs was more than the antelope could stomach. Speaking of stomachs, next time we'll put a window in Bossy's belly.

HUNTING PRONGHORN

The pronghorn's astonishing speed and superb vision are unmatched among North American big game animals. Hunters refer to pronghorns as antelope but they are not related to the antelope of Africa. They have no living relatives in the animal kingdom.

Pronghorns get their name from the sharp prongs that project forward on the horns of bucks. Their upper body is tan; the underside and rump white. Most antelope weigh 80 to 130 pounds, with the largest bucks weighing up to 140. Oregon's record pronghorn head has a right horn measuring 17-1/8 inches in length. Its left horn totals 17-3/8 inches long. The animal was shot in Harney County in 2000.

Hunting with Battle Creek Outfitters, Rodney Smith looked at several bucks before he made the stalk on this great pronghorn.

The fleet-footed pronghorn can reach a speed of 60 mph. An oversized windpipe and large lung capacity compared to their body size

Ed Boero used a muzzleloader to bag this nice pronghorn on a late summer hunt.

enable pronghorns to maintain high speeds for several miles. Their large, protruding eyeballs are approximately two inches in diameter and their vision is legendary.

Pronghorns prefer open plains, prairies and treeless foothills. The best habitat has rolling hills sprinkled with water holes and ample sagebrush for food. Pronghorns also eat forbs, brush and grasses. They feed heavily in early morning and late afternoon, but may graze anytime day or night. In the dry seasons of midsummer and fall they will go to a water hole at least once a day.

The pronghorn's sense of smell is good; however, sight and speed are their primary defenses. When alarmed, an antelope flares its white rump hairs or makes a barking sound, alerting others in the herd. Contrary, however, to their skittish nature, pronghorns are remarkably curious and may move a considerable distance to investigate an unusual sight.

In spring, mature dominant bucks claim territories that contain the best food and water. They vigorously defend the territory against other intruding bucks. As the rut approaches in August, the dominant or herd buck attempts to gather and keep a large harem of does in his territory, breeding each when they come into estrus. Pronghorn buck fights, as the herd buck chases intruding bucks away, seldom result in serious injury. These distractions may last long enough for a hunter to stalk within range.

Pronghorn bucks can be quickly identified by the black patches on cheeks and at the throat.

Spot-and-stalk is the primary tactic when hunting pronghorns. The hunter glasses, with binoculars or a spotting scope, from a high point of ground. After a good buck is spotted, a stalk, utilizing any available cover, is planned to

One study showed that the typical pronghorn diet consisted of 55% sagebrush, 30% rabbitbrush, 7% grass and 5% forbs (broadleaf plants).

get within shooting range.

Stand-hunting tactics can be used if a herd shows repeated daily movement patterns. Some hunters set up a blind and wait near a well-used waterhole or fence crossing. Pronghorns prefer to go under or through fences. They habitually cross at the same places, leaving hair on the barbed wire or on the ground. A stand near one of these crossing points can be productive.

PERPLEXING THE PRONGHORN It takes patience to hunt pronghorn. In Oregon, years of patience while you wait for the card to show up in the mail. When the season arrives, you've got just a few days to find the buck you're after. A few tricks in the bag can help close the deal on a buck. If you can perplex him and capitalize on his innate curiosity, you can get in position for the shot.

Good antelope country is not always good for hunting. Pronghorns stake their lives on phenomenal eyesight. On flat ground they are nearly unapproachable. Unless you resort to trickery.

Much of antelope country appears flat. Look closer and you will find washes, gullies and ditches that can be used for cover. Stream bottoms provide cover as well, sometimes in the form of trees. Fence posts, sagebrush and rocks can be all the cover you need.

When pronghorns are skittish, back off and watch from afar. If you can monitor the animals from late afternoon to dark, you can be reasonably sure to find them in the same place at first light.

If the animal you are after makes a dust trail for the state line, don't worry. Pronghorns like their home turf. He will be back. Find a spot with a clear view of a saddle, a wash or a river bottom that the antelope might use to return. They'll be back within an hour or three. Keep your rig out of sight, stay downwind and keep still.

It was patience that earned you your tag. A little more patience tempered with flexibility and the boldness of a confidence trickster can help you put antelope steaks in the freezer.

Final Approach

Late in the afternoon we sat on a ridge and watched a herd of wild horses. In the distance, I spotted a pronghorn. While we watched, he bedded beneath a juniper. I could see an approach through a rocky canyon. It would take two hours to get there through a mile of snake-infested, rocky ground with little cover except sagebrush, junipers and a deep canyon. The temperature hovered near 90 degrees. A fickle breeze blew from west to east.

This was one of the best bucks we'd seen in eight days of scouting and hunting. I dialed the Alpen scope up to 36-power and, through the hazy heat mirage, could see deep prongs and long horns that probably measured 14 inches or better.

"Do you want to go after him?"

Dara Smith took this great buck with her 7mm Remington Magnum and Nosler Ballistic Tips on the first day of a public land hunt.

Jerry asked.

I dumped out my daypack and put back what I needed. A compass, extra ammo, two knives and two bottles of water.

In full view, I walked at an angle across the open flat. Grasshoppers rattled in the dry grass. I stopped and changed direction when I heard a buzz that sounded like a rattlesnake.

Down in the junipers, I crept on hands and knees. To my left, I heard a snort and looked up the slope to see a lone buck with wide horns. He retreated north along the hillside. Above him, four wild horses trotted down, long tails and manes rippling. Two roan mares and a foal trailed behind a dappled gray stallion.

In the canyon, where I expected to find mule deer beds, I found horse trails, beaten down by unshod hooves, the underbrush gone. I was halfway up to the ridge top when Jerry honked the horn three times – our pre-arranged signal that meant something had spooked the animals.

It took a few minutes to locate the herd again. The horses had chased them a mile away. Now the buck was having a hard time with his girls. When his rival would move in to pick one off, the herd buck lowered his horns to drive him away. I watched four does head off up the slope. The buck had to circle around to head them back.

I watched him watch his rival, his does and the horses as he rested. I slipped out of sight and used junipers to close the distance. Somewhere ahead, between me and the herd buck, was the challenger.

If I spooked him, the game would be up. I eased from juniper to juniper down the hill. Still more than 600 yards away, I would be able to get no closer than 300 yards at best.

A movement caught my eye. The lone buck bolted into the open below me, then turned and lowered his horns. They stretched well beyond his ears, spread wide, almost like airplane wings. He took one hesitant step forward.

A decision to make. Six hundred yards out, beneath a lightning-struck juniper lay a big buck. And he had me pegged. One hundred yards away stood his rival.

With my sling wrapped around my forearm, I slipped the safety 'off,' steadied the crosshairs and squeezed the trigger. It had taken ten years to draw this tag and now the hunt was over. I'd have three miles to go across the hilltops, the meat heavy on my back. ■

Spot and stalk is the primary tactic when hunting pronghorns. The hunter glasses, with binoculars or a spotting scope, from a high point of ground. *Photo courtesy Carl Shaver*

Kenny Larkin AAMS
Branch Director
Vice President, Investments

Jared Larkin CFP®
Financial Advisor

Financial Services
RAYMOND JAMES
& ASSOCIATES, INC.
Member New York Stock Exchange/SIPC

Individual solutions from independent advisors.

222 NW 7th Street, Suite 2, Redmond, OR 97756
541-526-0507 • 541-526-0511 Fax
800-709-8977 Toll Free
www.larkinfinancial.com

ROCKY MOUNTAIN ELK

Sought after and prized for its magnificent antlers and tasty meat, a mature bull elk is one of the big game hunter's greatest trophies. A large animal may have antlers five feet long.

Rocky Mountain elk live east of the Cascade Mountains and prefer heavily-timbered country broken by clearcuts, burns, and meadows. The best habitat is in remote, mountainous terrain laced with streams and small glacial lakes. Elk also make their home in desert environs. In dry country, elk have large territories and will not tolerate human disturbance.

Cow elk live in large herds which also include calves and an occasional spike bull. An old cow leads the herd, alerting the others to danger with a sharp bark. Older bulls live alone or in small groups of up to six. Bulls wander more than cows, shunning cow herds until the mating season.

The breeding season or rut begins somewhere between late August and mid-September. Bulls break out of their summer bachelor herds and locate on ridgelines. A dominant bull, called a herd bull, bugles to advertise for a harem that may number up to 30 cows. He protects them from the advances of younger males, also called satellites, or of other herd bulls.

Cow elk hunts are a management tool ODFW uses to keep herd numbers in check and provide opportunity for hunters. *Photo courtesy Carl Shaver*

To detect danger, elk rely mainly on a keen sense of smell. They also have excellent hearing. On windy days, when swishing tree limbs would obscure the sound of a hunter's approach, they become nervous and retreat to heavy cover. Elk quickly notice movement, but usually ignore stationary objects.

An elk can run 35 mph in a short burst and can maintain a 15 to 20 mph trot over a long distance. A running bull carries his nose high, so his antlers lay back along his body and do not tangle in branches. Elk are strong swimmers and can jump obstructions up to 10 feet high.

Elk feed mainly on grasses. As winter nears, they consume more browse, the twigs and leaves from shrubs and trees. The morning feeding period begins about one hour before sunrise and lasts until one hour after. In late afternoon, they begin feeding about two hours before sunset and continue until dark. Elk usually have four or five shorter feeding periods during the day, each lasting from 15 minutes to one hour.

One of the most productive techniques is stand-hunting in early morning and late afternoon. Especially when the stand is on or near a saddle that the elk use to move between one drainage and the next.

Because they eat so often, elk usually bed within a mile of where they feed. They prefer bedding areas with a good view, like a grassy terrace or bench about ¾ of the way up on a hillside.

In summer and early fall, elk scatter over a large area at high elevation. The rugged terrain prevents intrusion by humans. In late fall, heavy snow and extreme cold push elk to lower elevations. But with a break in the weather, they may return to high altitudes. Some herds move 100 miles to find the right conditions.

HUNTING FOR ELK Elk don't come easy. A successful elk hunter must earn his trophy. Unlike most other big game animals, elk will retreat deep

The work isn't done when the season opens. Chances are you'll be at least two miles from the road when you find the herd. Pray you spot the bull before he fades back into the timber.

into the forest or climb to extreme elevations to escape hunting pressure.

> **Scouting is the variable that sets the consistently successful hunter apart from the merely lucky and the folks that go home empty-handed most years.**

Learn the escape cover where elk go to hide during the season. When the season opens, hunt open country and watch well-traveled trails. On day two or three, turn your attention to those deep, dark

Rocky Mountain Elk in Eastern Oregon

Oregon's Rocky Mountain elk are found from the western slope of the Cascades, all the way to the Idaho border. Elk are often associated with the forests of northeast Oregon and south central Oregon, but large numbers of elk make their living in the sage and junipers of the high desert throughout southeast Oregon.

General elk bow and controlled bow seasons begin at the end of August and provide up to four weeks in the field. Bag limits are set to meet management objectives in specific units. Controlled hunts are held to promote opportunity and trophy quality and also to minimize damage complaints on agricultural lands. The general first season and second season hunts in late October and November provide opportunities for rifle hunters who were unsuccessful in the controlled hunt lottery.

The success of the Rocky Mountain elk in Oregon and around the West is a tribute to far-sighted sportsmen, who in the early 1900s, pushed for legislation to protect them from over-hunting. Foremost was President Theodore Roosevelt, who was instrumental in setting aside crucial habitat so that future generations would be able to see and hunt elk in the wild.

Today, organizations like the Oregon Hunters Association and the Rocky Mountain Elk Foundation keep the spirit alive, with efforts to promote conservation and enhance wildlife habitat.

For more information on hunting elk in Oregon, visit the Department of Fish and Wildlife web site at www.dfw.state.or.us/resources/hunting/big_game.

Battle Creek Outfitters
Mule Deer, Rocky Mountain Elk, & Wild Turkey hunts in Eastern Oregon's best game country.

Steve Mathers
&
Mike Crawford

541-389-0743
www.BattleCreekOutfitters.com

Elk usually have four or five shorter feeding periods during the day, each lasting from 15 minutes to one hour. Because they eat so often, elk usually bed within a mile of where they feed.

hideaways that you marked in the preseason.

Though some hunters may tag out on the first day, most will spend six days or more in the field. In seasons that are limited to five days, you will need to spend a day or two of extra scouting to compensate.

Plan to spend several days on the hunt. Scout a prospective area to find fresh elk sign then set up camp at least a mile away.

Scent can help a hunter locate areas used by elk. The animals emit a strong, musky odor and the scent lingers in bedding or wallowing areas long after the elk leave.

One of the most productive techniques is stand-hunting in early morning and late afternoon. Especially when the stand is on or near a saddle that the elk use to move between one drainage and the next. For a morning hunt, walk to your stand in the dark, moving quietly to avoid spooking any elk in the vicinity. Remain on your stand until about two hours after sunrise, glassing to find elk that you

Guns and Loads for Elk

The hunter contemplating an elk rifle should know that, while even the .243 Winchester is legal for elk, the best choice is a bigger caliber. Elk often run when shot. Bigger bullets make bigger holes and a good blood trail makes following a wounded animal a lot easier.

Elk are bigger-boned than blacktails or mule deer. It takes a heavier bullet to put an elk down with one shot.

For a dedicated elk gun, consider a .270 Winchester or larger. If shots may be cross-canyon, use a rifle and load with flatter trajectory over long distances.

For younger hunters or the recoil-sensitive, a 7mm-.08 is a good option. Use the 140-grain bullet. The 7mm Magnum and 7mm Winchester Short Magnum offer a step up in performance with the 160-grain projectile.

The .30-.06 Springfield is an excellent choice. It can be loaded with bullets ranging in weight to 220 grains. One great choice is Nosler's AccuBond. The 165-grain bonded bullet has an excellent ballistic coefficient and is strong enough to penetrate and break bone.

The .300 Winchester Magnum, the .300 Winchester Short Magnum, the .325 WSM, the .338 Winchester Magnum and the .35 Whelen are great for punching to the vitals and putting an elk down in a hurry.

THE PATENTED GAME WINCH
- Fits any pickup truck
- One person can load any animal
- Extremely portable
SIX EASY STEPS

541-480-1536
thegamewinch@gmail.com

could stalk. In the afternoon, be on your stand at least two hours before sunset.

In midday, when elk are bedded down, you are more likely to see them by still-hunting. The technique works best when the ground is damp or covered with soft snow. Noise doesn't spook the elk as much as scent does. Use scent control to keep the human odor in check.

A drive can be effective, but only if the hunting

Topographic Maps for the Elk Hunter

Topography, as defined by Random House Dictionary, is "the art of describing on maps and charts the physical features of an area, as mountains and rivers." Elk season is not the time to skimp. A hunter needs detail and resolution and they are found on the 7.5 Minute Series, 1:24000 scale U.S. Geological Survey maps. These maps are also called quadrangles or quads and they are indispensable for pre-scouting, scouting and the hunt.

With the contour intervals of 40 feet on a 7.5 minute topo, it is easy to pinpoint the biggest roadless areas, identify swamps, scope out north-facing ridges and find most of the springs and even some of the seeps. With a good topo, it's easy to identify the south-facing slopes where elk find warmth in the winter and the north-faces where elk go to cool in the summer heat.

It may take more than one topo to cover all of an elk herd's potential range. To locate a particular river canyon, follow the river downstream to the next map. The name of the next map is found by looking at the edge of the chart. At the boundary, in parentheses is the name, which usually refers to some major terrain feature such as a mountain or a lake.

party is familiar with the terrain. Drivers approach from below a known bedding area and push the elk uphill to posters. The posters station themselves along game trails in thick timber or near clearings where elk are likely to break into the open. A startled elk will make plenty of noise. But more often, they slip away silently, so posters must watch closely.

During breeding activity, which can take place between late August and early November, elk sounds can bring elk within range. Bull sounds are most often used in archery season when fights between bulls are common. If a herd bull answers but does not move, he is probably guarding his harem and reluctant to leave. In this case, try to stalk close enough for a shot.

Cow and calf sounds may be effective throughout the season to mimic herd noises and call bulls and cows. ■

Elk feed mainly on grasses. As winter nears, they consume more browse-the twigs and leaves from shrubs and trees. *Photo courtesy Matt Smith*

ROOSEVELT ELK
By Scott Haugen

Five hours into day six of the hunt, the bull I'd been after finally came into view. Minutes prior I'd passed up a fair 6x6 inside 20 yards, and didn't want to regret it. The way the big bull was moving, the situation looked promising.

I first saw the dark-racked, heavy-framed bull a day prior, but despite his aggressive bugling, he wouldn't leave his harem. Though he answered my seductive cow calls, he just wouldn't budge. When I tried stalking in on him, the cows busted me and it was over.

But this was another day, and the situation different. I found the bull 200 yards from his harem, having just run off a challenger bull. My target bull gathered his cows and headed down the ridge, through a brushy draw and up on to the hillside on which I stood. Though they were nearly a mile away, I felt I had a chance.

By the time I stalked into position, his herd had joined another, and now there were over 30 sets of eyeballs to contend with. This time my cow calls worked, but the wrong bulls kept coming in. Not wanting to get busted by calling in lesser bulls and letting them go, I shut-up.

An hour later, after a tedious stalk, I was within 75 yards of my target bull. When he disappeared behind some brush, on the trail of some cows, I cut the distance. The moment the first cow hit the opening, I ranged her and got ready.

As soon as the bull waltzed into the clearing, he looked even bigger than I'd expected. His dark mane, massive, chiseled body and confident stride left no doubt he was the big bull on the block. A few more steps into the open and I let out a cow call. The instant the bull stopped, my arrow was on its way. Soon I was admiring my best Roosevelt bull taken

In early summer, hunters on scouting trips may find bulls grouped together in bachelor herds.

with bow and arrow.

During that September hunt along Oregon's central coast, I was in elk every day, and learned a lot. I've been fortunate to hunt many parts of Oregon–even the world–and consider tagging a mature Roosevelt elk the second most challenging

In late summer and early fall, elk may be found scattered over large areas at higher elevations. Scott Haugen with a big Roosevelt bull.

animal to hunt in all of North America, second only to the cagey Columbia blacktail deer.

Oregon's Roosevelt elk season typically commences around September 1st, with archery season. Most coastal Roosevelt archery tags can be purchased over the counter, and there is no quota. However, there are some prized, limited-draw areas where archers have the opportunity to rewrite the record books should they draw a tag and have the endurance to tackle the demanding terrain.

Archers can also hunt the west side of the Cascades for what are dubbed Cascade Roosevelts. These are elk that can breed with Rocky Mountain elk; that's not to say they do, but given the migrations, it's possible.

Hunters seeking a pure-strain Roosevelt for the record books will want to focus efforts west of I-5.

I'm not saying the east side of the Cascades doesn't have pure-blood Roosevelts, it does, especially in the lower elevations and namely the surrounding foothills and valley floors. There are some monster, pure-strain Roosy's being taken from low in the Cascades every year, but if you want to put them into a record book, they'll have to go under the Cascades Roosevelt category.

Once the September bow season closes, rifle hunters looking for Roosevelts have only the Cascades in which to hunt. The season is usually short—normally a week—and tags can be bought over the counter. In November, two rifle hunts open in the Coast Range, and again, tags can be acquired over the counter.

There are also several opportunities for hunters to draw highly prized tags through the state's annual lottery system. These limited-draw tags offer the highest percentage opportunity at finding a trophy bull, then again, world-class Roosevelts can pop-up anywhere in their historic range. There are also several limited-draw cow tags available, some with lengthy seasons, and don't forget extra management tags that are often distributed through regional ODF&W offices helping control crop damaged areas.

The current world-record Roosevelt was taken on the floor of the Willamette Valley, during an August rifle hunt. It was the first Roosevelt taken by a hunter to ever score over 400 inches. There are many limited-draw units that kick-out big bulls, and the opportunities seem to only keep increasing for hunters, along with the elk's growing population.

Some units, like the Tioga and Saddle Mountain, carry antler restrictions of 3-point or better. Units like this are home to some giant bulls, but just because there's an antler restriction in place, don't think elk will be hiding behind every tree.

Due to the dense, jungle-like habitat Roosevelt elk call home, hunting them is a great physical and mental challenge. I've seen many hunters from outside the West wince when they simply lay eyes on the rugged Coast Range. Some of my most demanding hunts on the planet have taken place in these mountains.

The McKenzie Unit produced this 6x7 Cascade bull for hunter Jessica Matthews.

Figuring out how to best hunt Roosevelts is just like hunting any other big game; you must first know what the animals are doing during the time of year you plan on hunting them.

In early September, archers set their sights on love-sick bulls. This is the time of the rut where anything can happen. While the use of cow calls and bugles are the main ways hunters try to bring elk to within bow range, spot-and-stalk tactics should not be overlooked. On hot, early September days, sitting in treestands along trails connecting bedding and watering or feeding areas, can be very productive.

When calling Roosevelt bulls, be patient, for they

are notorious for coming in silent. I don't know how many times bulls have come in quiet to my calls and I've not heard or seen them until they were within spitting distance. This is far different from how Rocky Mountain bulls usually respond.

Once you've done your homework and know bulls are in the area, don't give up calling. More times than I care to admit, I've called, given up after 20 minutes of seeing nothing, only to return to the exact spot minutes later and see bulls standing right there. There's no set rule as to how these bulls will respond to calls, or how they will react. Patience, persistence and time in the woods are the best teaching tools.

Look for bulls to shed their velvet sometime in late August. The breeding season or rut begins somewhere between late August and mid-September. Breeding activity may continue into November.

If you hear bulls responding to your calls, but they're not coming any closer, don't give up. Instead, get the wind in your face and slowly walk your way into the herd while simultaneously using cow and calf calls. Cows and calves are very vocal this time of year, and they make lots of noise when walking through the dry forest. Use the natural sounds of cracking brush, calf and cow sounds to your advantage and you might have your season end sooner rather than later.

The rut will extend through all of the September bow season, with many hunters feeling the best action comes the third week of the month. Like the rut calendars of other game, the peak of the Roosevelt rut can vary from year to year, even from drainage to drainage.

Just because bow season ends doesn't mean the bulls are done rutting. Some rifle hunters have discovered the value of using calls during the state's general season in the Cascades. While bulls may not come to a call, they will often bugle, giving away their

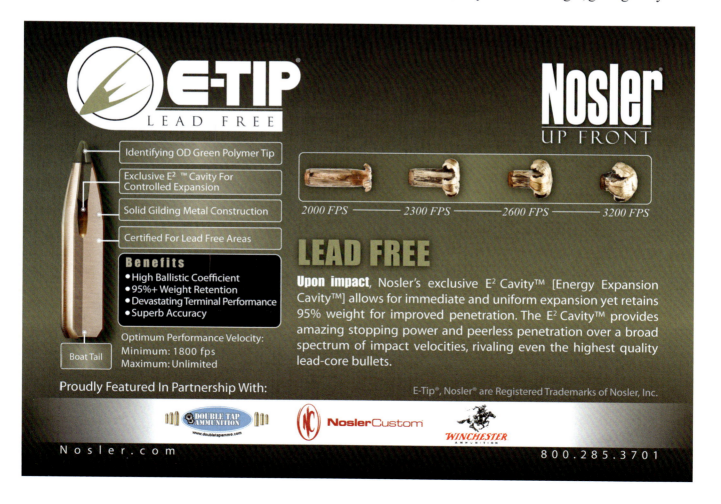

whereabouts.

Spot-and-stalk is the most popular way to rifle hunt for Roosevelts, no matter the time of year. Typically, elk can be spotted on the edges of logged units, browsing early and late in the day. Play the wind and carefully plan your stalk. If, at any time an elk winds you, the gig is up. I've never had an elk smell me and hold still long enough for a shot.

If the herd–or bachelor group of bulls–is moving in a specific direction, you can often get in front of them, placing yourself in optimal shooting position. However, the norm is for the elk to feed on the edges of a unit, not far from timber. Once they're done, they duck back into the timber for the day. But just because they're in the timber–normally in the bottom of the biggest, deepest canyon–doesn't mean they're untouchable.

Many seasoned hunters prefer chasing Roosevelt bulls in the timber. By mid-October, rains have usually quieted the forest floor, and winds are more consistent. Though shots may come at close range, nothing hones your hunting skills like tracking elk through the forest. Once a big bull track is found, follow it. I believe this is the biggest lost art in all of elk hunting; finding a track and following it until the deal is done. There are some monster bulls living in the deep, wet forest that have never been seen by a human, and they avoid road-hunters like the plague. Take to the woods with the intent of tracking down a bull, and you just may find what you've always dreamed of.

James Flaherty with a five-point Cascade Roosevelt bull he called in on a solo last-day hunt.

Come the November general coast seasons, Roosevelt bulls live each day with the goal of amassing as much food as possible in preparation for winter, and avoiding predators. While the rut deprives their bodies of fat reserves, the bulls are lucky to have enough food on which to feed before it starts losing it's nutritional value later in the winter.

At this time–and most times–the bulls are largely home bodies. Roosevelts won't travel far because they don't have to. The climate is mild in the Coast Range, and all the food, water and shelter is in one spot, meaning the elk don't need to migrate like their Rocky Mountain cousins do. While bulls may move up or down a drainage, this is not to be confused with a migration, it's not. It's just a simple shift usually caused by a need for food or increased pressure by fellow hunters.

Typically, once a wise Roosy bull is spooked, he'll remain in the same area and go into hiding where even the best of hunters likely won't find him. Their movements become very restricted and deliberate, sticking close to their core area and never far from cover.

Many elk take up living in thick reprod units, which are almost impossible to hunt alone. This is where organizing a hunting party can pay off. Strategically place a couple of hunters on stands, then have the others driving the brush with the hopes of pushing out the elk for a shot. When conducting drives, be sure everyone is wearing bright orange so they can be seen easily.

Whether you hold a general season Roosevelt tag, or one of the prized limited-draw tags, the key to success is understanding elk behavior. The next step is figuring out how the elk behave within their brushy, intimidating habitat. From there, it's a matter of being mentally tough, physically prepared and doing what's necessary to put meat in the freezer. These elk are far from easy to hunt, which makes them one of Oregon's greatest big game animals to pursue.

BIGHORN SHEEP

Blackpowder Bighorn on Beatys Butte

Sykes put down the phone and told his customers he had to go outside. He shut the door and stepped out into the alley. Here, with no one to see him, he did his happy dance.

He'd made the phone call to the Oregon Department of Fish and Wildlife to check on the results of his tag applications and learned he'd drawn hunt No. 570C for bighorn sheep in Oregon's controlled hunt lottery.

A bighorn sheep hunt is thought by many to be the most expensive game of all. At auctions, bids of $200,000 or more are not unheard-of. A desert sheep hunt in Mexico will run you $50,000 and a stone sheep hunt in Canada will cost $30,000. But any Oregon hunter could draw a bighorn tag this year and it doesn't have to take a life's savings to make the hunt of a lifetime.

In the drawing, odds average about 1 in 200 for a bighorn tag. For that once-in-a-lifetime hunt, an Oregon resident will pay only $101.50.

An Oregon bighorn tag comes along once in a lifetime. Sykes Mitchell opted to use a muzzleloader on his hunt.

Sykes bought his tag then began an intense regimen with a personal trainer. With three months to go, he picked up the telephone and rang every biologist who had ever worked in the Beatys Butte unit. Each time he got a tip, he marked it on his map.

As patterns began to emerge on paper, Sykes planned his scouting trips. For the next few weeks, every chance he had, he packed his family into the truck and headed south on the six-hour drive into the desert.

Most experts recommend a flat-shooting rifle for a sheep hunt, but Sykes was determined to make every aspect of the hunt as hard as possible. He chose a 54-caliber Lyman Great Plains Rifle. Shooting a patched round ball, he'd have to be close. And that was just how he wanted it.

Opening day, the mood was electric. With a team of friends in camp to continue the scouting, Sykes and John Williams headed back to the spot where, two days before, Sykes had located two big rams.

At mid-morning, the hunters found a herd of ewes and

lambs. They moved a half-mile to see the sheep from a different angle, and finally, three rams came into view. One of them was a big one.

Williams had his binoculars up. "That's him. That's the one," he said, reaching for his rangefinder. From their vantage point, the sheep were now less than a hundred yards away.

Sykes slipped the rifle from his case. "Just keep telling me how far out he is," he whispered. "I haven't loaded my rifle yet."

With practiced hands, he reached into his possibles bag. Pour in the powder. Pack it down. Put a patch on the barrel . . .

Sykes looked up. The ram was standing alert now, nervous. Sykes' hands began to tremble. Shaking now, he got the round ball out and put it on the patch. With a starter, he pushed it down. In two strokes, he had rammed it on the powder.

He grabbed the shooting sticks and the rams began to move. "One hundred-five," Williams whispered. "One-oh-eight." He took his sheep call from his pocket.

Sykes eared back the hammer and pinched a No. 11 cap on the nipple.

"One-fifteen." The rams were trotting now. Williams blew on his call. The sheep halted, but Sykes wasn't ready.

"One-eighteen." Williams sounded the call one more time, dropped it and punched the button on his rangefinder. "One-twenty-four."

Sykes was on the ground now, his rifle in the web of the shooting sticks, his right leg doubled beneath him, left leg bent for support. The big ram had stopped and was looking back. Broadside, but his horn covered his vitals.

Sykes stroked the set trigger. Click. He put the pad of his index against the hair trigger as he'd done so many times in practice. When the ram swung his head back uphill, his shoulder was exposed and the hunter applied the last pound of pressure to the trigger.

When the smoke cleared, Sykes climbed up to his ram alone. He reached down and touched the horn, traced the curl and the growth rings and ran his fingers through the hair. His three-month journey from happy dance to harvest had come down to a split-second decision to shoot. But he knew it had been a team effort that put him in position behind the shooting sticks.

When the head was scored, the horns measured 168-1/8 inches using the Boone and Crockett system with a final score of 158. Sykes had taken the trophy of a lifetime on public land in Oregon's high desert.

Defying the odds, A.J. Conte drew a bighorn sheep tag. A Nosler Partition connected the young hunter with his trophy. When measured later, the growth rings proved that the animal was 4-1/2 years old. *Photo by Tyler Saunders*

Harry Caron with his Hart Mountain bighorn. *Photo courtesy Gene Caron*

And he did it the hard way.

Each year, approximately 90 bighorn tags are awarded in Oregon's big-game drawing. The deadline for application is May 15. Maybe next year is your year.

ROCKY MOUNTAIN GOAT

In the Throne Room of the Mountain King

The quest for a trophy goat in northeast Oregon, at the top of the world

He climbed by the light of the moon, careful to make little noise in these last minutes before dawn. But in the darkness, he took a wrong turn and found himself against a wall. "I'd think, 'Find a little handhold and then find a place for my foot and then find another handhold and I'll keep going.' I was about a half-mile from where I should have gone up."

By sunrise, Darrel Ries clung to the face of a mountain on a narrow ledge carved from the granite by wind, rain and snow. He was out of handholds and there was no way down. "I had just a two-foot ledge I could sit on. I had enough room for my feet to be in front of me and my arm back in the hole behind me. I was holding on for dear life. I don't even like to be on a ladder."

8,571 hunters applied for one of Oregon's Rocky Mountain goat tags in 2008. One of the lucky eight was 53-year-old Darrel Ries, a chiropractor from Bend, Oregon. With three months to get ready, Paulina Peak, in central Oregon, became his training ground. The three-mile hike gains 2,000 feet, close to what he was likely to encounter in goat country.

In a straight line, Cusick Mountain is 11 miles south from Wallowa Lake. The trail from the lake is shorter, but it is steep with switchbacks where one stirrup hangs out over thin air. The

Darrel Ries used a 7mm Weatherby Magnum to take this trophy billy in northeast Oregon. Mountain goat country, as rugged as it is breathtaking, pushed the 53-year-old to his limits. "It was just an incredible adventure in beautiful country. It really got to the point where taking a goat was secondary to the whole trip." Photo courtesy Darrel Ries

longer trail follows the Imnaha River and has its own share of switchbacks, but the elevation change is spread out.

Darrel swung into the saddle on a September morning. With him were Russ Morris, of La Grande, and Ron (Bino) Bennett, from Portland, and the outfitter, whose job it was to deposit hunters and camp in a meadow, then return eight days later to pick them up.

Both Russ and Bino were veterans of past triathlons. Bino's mountain climbing skills were to prove helpful.

The pack string followed the middle fork of the Imnaha River, up, up, up. Once above a pool, hundreds of miles from the ocean, Ries looked down to see two salmon in the clear water. The riders picked their way along cliff walls and crevasses that dropped hundreds of feet. At one switchback, Ries's rifle case slipped off the mule and tumbled to the rocks below.

Inside were two scoped rifles. Ries couldn't help but wonder if one or both of the scopes had been jarred in the fall. In the high country, the trail flattened out and they passed a large burn then skirted Marble Mountain to a meadow at the base of Cusick Mountain.

Ries had one day to scout. In the morning, he saw "an enormous goat." His body was massive, his hair yellow and longer than the other goats." The big billy's horns were visibly bigger, even a mile-and-a-half away.

As the three men watched, the King fed across the granite cliff and disappeared into a rock formation they dubbed 'the throne.'

"Every day we saw five to ten goats," Ries said. "We figured they came down the mountain to feed in the meadows after dark and returned to the cliffs at sunrise."

It took an hour-and-a-half to reach his stand in the dark. When the sun came up, he stripped off his backpack and coat, left them behind and climbed higher.

A group of goats moved up the side of the mountain. Ries thought the King was with them, but for 45 minutes, another goat kept Ries pinned down, unable to move. Ries shivered too much to make a shot. Soon, all the goats were out of sight. Ries followed their trail up and over the top.

Back at camp, Russ and Bino worried. Bino climbed the mountain, found Reis's backpack and assumed the worst. Russ and Bino began to search for a body in the canyons below. Ries found his 'rescuers' minutes before they called for help on the satellite phone.

Before dawn on day two, free-climbing with his rifle and 30-pound pack, Ries ran out of options on a narrow ledge. He couldn't go up or down. He reached Russ on the radio. It took Russ an hour to locate the chiropractor hanging on by his fingers.

Two hours later, Bino climbed around Ries and tied one end of a 200-foot rope to a twisted hemlock. "Ten feet above was a gnarled tree stuck in the rock. I didn't know if it would hold us or not." Bino gave Ries the harness and then tied his own out of rope. Then Bino showed Ries how to rappel down the cliff.

On the third day, on the backside of the mountain, the big billy was in range. Ries found a rest and missed, his bullet hit high over the animal's back. Later he realized he forgot to compensate for the angle, but he put his 338 Winchester Magnum back in the case and carried his 7mm Weatherby Magnum.

On the fourth day the team saw a group of goats on the mountain. One of the young goats tumbled 200 yards down the hillside. It lay still. For a few minutes, the nanny watched. Finally the group moved off. About an hour later, the kid got up, shook himself and joined the rest of the group.

Every year, the State of Oregon issues 10 tags for Rocky Mountain goats in northeast Oregon. Most of the hunts are so remote and require such an investment in time that some hunters, having drawn the tag, stay home. Scott Tibbs, of Prineville, OR, tagged his trophy billy on the second day of his hunt.

On the fifth day, there were no goats to be seen from camp. Ries crept over the snow at the ridge top, looked into the next basin and saw seven goats. Startled, they took off at a run. Russ and Bino located the group with two billies at the top of the next ridge.

Neither of the two males was the King but Ries made a decision to shoot. 321 yards. He settled in behind the rifle, centered the crosshair. The bullet spanged rock, but the goat took five steps and stopped. Ries held low for the second shot.

The hunter found a narrow trail to his white-robed trophy. At the top of the world, he ran his fingers in the long hair and looked out across snow-capped peaks that stretched in every direction.

When Russ and Bino joined him, they removed the hide and divided meat into packs, cooled with snow from the canyon. That night, under the light of a full moon, they feasted on backstrap.

Somewhere on the mountain, flat rocks shifted beneath hardened hooves and shale creaked like broken glass. Between knife-edged black granite and darkened sky, the King was secure in his throne. ■

FERAL SWINE

Hooves thundered on the hillside, black shadows in the trees. I scrambled up the slope and focused on a spot ahead of where I'd seen the herd. If I figured right, they'd appear in a window in the oaks. I steadied my Winchester against a tree.

The first hog into the open was a big sow, the rest were a blur of black bodies, flashing single-file through the trunks of the oaks that grew thicker than cloves on a Christmas ham.

With my crosshairs bracketed one-third of the way up the body on the biggest animals, I waited for a good shot. A dozen pigs passed, then two small oinkers flashed into and out of sight. The next was bigger, its nose now in view . My brain told my trigger finger, 'Now!' The rifle bucked and a 160-grain Nosler AccuBond found its mark 85 yards up the hill. Five more pigs rumbled by, then all was quiet.

This California porker was at the back of a long line of sows and pigs running full tilt for cover.

I found the pig ten yards farther on, a 110-pound sow, probably six months old, packing plenty of lean, organic pork loin and chops.

That California hog hunt on a Wilderness Unlimited ranch was my first true wild boar experience and I've had several since, in California, Hawaii and Oregon.

These aren't agricultural oinkers. Adult wild hogs tip the scales between 100 and 200 pounds. Boars can reach 375 or more. Most European/feral crosses have a coat of long, coarse, dark hair. Boars grow wicked tusks and are not the kind of critters you'd like to run into on a narrow trail.

They feed mainly at night. They eat everything from acorns to alfalfa, to rattlesnakes and bird

Two signs of hog activity – rooting for grubs and dried mud on the side of the tree where a big boar scratched.

eggs. At dawn, they head for the deepest, darkest cover they can find.

They multiply. Starting at six months old, a sow can produce piglets at the rate of two litters per year. That adds up to a lot of pork on the ground and less habitat for deer and elk.

Feral hogs have been found in the John Day River watershed near Ashwood and Antelope north of Madras. Swine have also been seen on the loose near the communities of Spray and Kimberly and near Post and Paulina in Crook County. Rumor has it that there are feral swine in the Siskiyous in southern Oregon.

OTHER EXOTICS Herds of feral sheep, exotic deer and goats make their home in various parts of the state, mainly on private land. It is important that the hunter make the distinction between true feral animals and animals that may be the property of a rancher. Always obtain permission before hunting on private land.

A few herds of feral sheep are remnant in river canyons of eastern Oregon. This nice mouflon ram was taken from a herd of about 30 sheep east of Fossil.

WHERE TO HUNT

When many landowners are limiting access to private land and more hunters compete for a finite resource on public lands, good information helps the hunter know where to locate game and where to apply to maximize the potential of drawing good tags.

Every year there are a few hunts which are under-subscribed; hunts that are good bets where success often runs high. Sometimes it means that the hunter must use a bow or a shotgun or a muzzleloader instead of a rifle. Sometimes it means hunting solo when tags are limited.

Start the search by reading. It helps to be familiar with the *Oregon Big Game Regulations* and, in particular, the unit maps. Controlled hunts are listed in tables showing hunt number, hunt name, bag limit, season dates and number of tags that were offered in the previous year. This tells part of the story.

The hunt descriptions that follow the tables tell the boundaries of the hunt area and the percentage of public lands. From this you get some idea of your chances of drawing a tag and the possibilities of finding a place to hunt.

Next, turn to the *Oregon Tag Guide* for Controlled Hunt Drawing Odds. The tables in this book list percentage of public land, hunt number and name and historical harvest percentages. The tables show just what the likely chances of drawing a tag for a particular hunt under Oregon's preference point system.

The *Oregon Hunter* magazine put out by the Oregon Hunters Association is another good resource to help the hunter locate new ground. Other good sources include *Washington-Oregon Game & Fish* magazine and *Northwest Sportsman*. These periodicals regularly spotlight productive hunting units.

Another good source of information is the *Record Book for Oregon's Big Game*, now in its fourth edition.

After you have narrowed the search to a particular area, start talking to real people. Ask hunters you know for the names of others who have hunted your unit. Contact ODFW biologists. The numbers and addresses for the regional offices are located in the back of this book. Ask for the names and contact information for the field biologists responsible for your unit. Find out how animals fared during the previous winter, ask about predation and buck-to-doe or bull-to-cow ratios. Also ask about recent logging operations and road closures.

Many ODFW employees are hunters. Don't expect them to tell you where they hunt, but it doesn't hurt to ask where they might consider trying.

Contrary to what some would have you believe, much of the best hunting in our state is still on public land. Start with a map that shows the whole unit and then identify areas of public land. Bureau of Land Management maps, readily available, give this information.

Look for roadless areas and identify where agricultural

lands give way to forest where forest gives way to desert. Locate a few possible pockets where deer, elk or antelope can find food, water, shelter and escape cover. Now you need the detail you can find on a topographical map.

With a topo map, showing larger scale, you can identify water sources and 'edge' habitat. Look for saddles and natural avenues of travel that game might use. Now a scouting trip is in order.

Go at least a couple of weeks before the season starts. Walk the trails and watch for sign and make notes on your topo map.

Once the season starts, don't quit asking questions and seeking information. Consistent success comes to those who make their own luck by learning all they can about the area and the big game they pursue. ■

WHERE TO HUNT - WESTERN UNITS

WESTERN UNITS

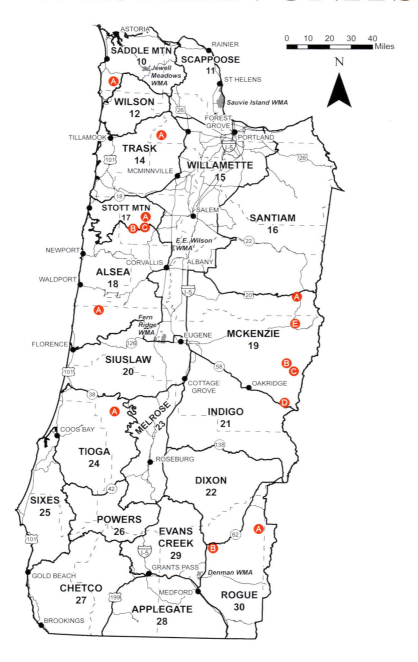

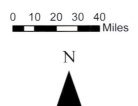

EASTERN UNITS

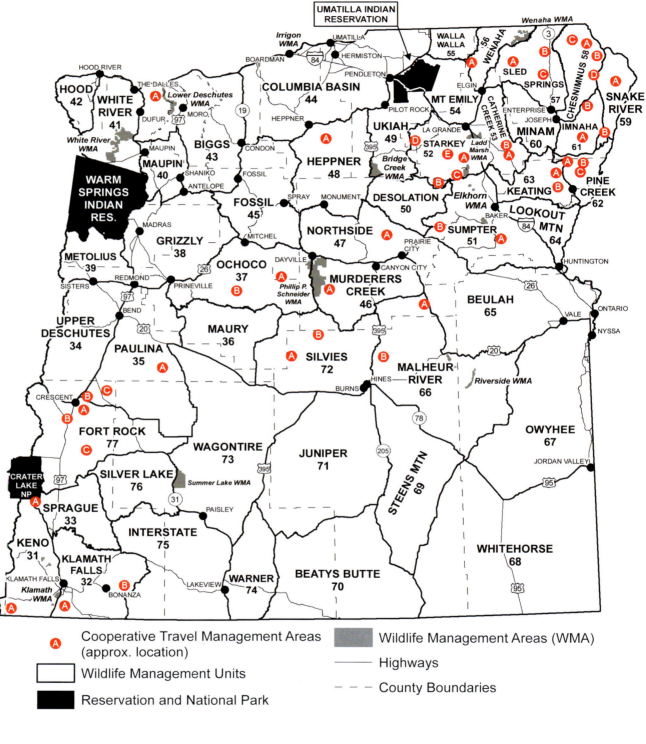
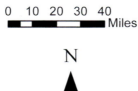

KNIVES

Which knife I choose is dependent on the work I intend to do. A fixed blade is best for heavy chores like cutting branches out of a shooting lane, cutting rope or whittling a fire starter. If I need a blade that can double as a pry bar then it is the fixed blade that I want.

A folder is a better choice when it comes to a small game or a bird hunt. It is lighter and it takes up less space.

If we are hunting big game I choose a fixed blade. To my way of thinking there is no more efficient method to bring out meat than to leave bones and offal in the field. A lot of knives can be put to work, but some are better suited to the task.

A fixed blade is faster than any folder, which is apt to be left in the pack or buried beneath cartridges and keys. It should be just big enough for the job, and ride close to hand, on the strong-side hip behind the belt loop so it can slide way to the small of the back.

Bird hunting is entirely different. The knife I carry on a dove hunt or a pheasant hunt is a light, single-blade folder with a 2-1/2-inch blade.

On a folding knife, a locking blade is far safer and will give you much more pleasing service than a knife's blade that doesn't lock.

For most hunting work, a blade length between three and five inches is sufficient. For a knife that will see heavy duty beyond gutting and skinning, another inch or two will help as longer knives usually have stouter blades.

A knife used for cleaning big game needs to have a handle that can be grasped and held without turning in the hand under heavy pressure. Your hands may be sweaty or cold, wet or bloody or some combination. For this reason I like a stouter handle that I can hold onto, one that spans the palm of my hand, slab-sided of wood or textured rubber.

A small game blade sees less stress and therefore a light, strong plastic handle or a thin wood handle is more than adequate.

A good knife is worth little unless it is kept clean and sharp. Keep a spare blade or a sharpening stone nearby when cleaning big game and take a few swipes on the stone after each brace of quail.

I use a sheet of paper to test an edge. If I hold the blade at the end of the paper and a gentle sawing motion slices through it, I know my knife is sharp enough for any job I require it to do. ◾

A custom knife from Three Sisters Forge in Bend, Oregon.

RIFLES & CARTRIDGES

Hunters should choose their big-game tool with care. It should be the appropriate caliber for the game, carry well and fit the hunter comfortably. Some shooters are sensitive to recoil and the hunter should choose a gun that he or she can shoot without flinching.

.22 centerfire rifles, such as the .223 or the .22-.250 Remington, are legal for deer hunting in Oregon but they are not the best choice for deer-sized game. The .243 Winchester or 6mm Remington is the best place to start for someone who hunts deer and antelope but also would like to use their gun for varmints such as rockchucks and coyotes. Bullet size is key. You can buy bullets for these guns in a range from 55 grains on up to 105 grains. The smaller bullets can be propelled at speeds up to 4000 feet per second (fps) and should be considered as varmint loads. The heavier bullets, 85 grains and up, are better all-around bullets for coyotes, deer and antelope.

Today's modern sporting rifles are another step in the evolution of the tools hunters and target shooters use to enjoy the shooting sports.

A solid rest beats an offhand shot every time. Rest your weak hand or elbow on a solid object like a tree limb or rock. Do not rest your rifle directly on the object.

In Oregon it is legal to use any caliber larger than .24 for elk. And there are a few hunters who rely on the .243 or the .257 Roberts and such guns as their primary rifle for elk but these are probably not the best choices for an elk gun. The .270 Winchester is a good compromise between the high-speed, smaller bullets and big bores of .30 caliber or larger. The .270 can be loaded with bullets from around 130 grains to 160 grains. This is a caliber that is perfect for thin-skinned animals such as antelope and deer. It is good for sheep, goats and bear and adequate for elk.

The 7mm Remington Magnum brings a step up in performance from the .270 but with it comes a step up in recoil. The 7mm (.284 caliber) Rem Mag can be loaded from 120 grains up to 175.

The .30-.06 Springfield loaded with a 150-grain bullet is an excellent all-around choice for any game encountered in our state. It can be loaded with bullets ranging in weight from 110 grains to 220. The 150- to 165-grain bullets are excellent deer and antelope loads and an elk hunter should consider using 180 grain bullets for elk.

For elk, the .300 Win Mag, the .338, the .350 Rem Mag and the .35 Whelen are great for reaching the vitals and putting an elk down in a hurry.

The hunter who needs a rifle for pursuing bear specifically should know that, while the .22 centerfires are legal for bear in Oregon, the best choice is a bigger caliber. Bear will run when shot and their long hair can soak up a lot of blood. Quite simply, bigger bullets make bigger holes and a good blood trail makes following the bear a lot easier. Consider the .30 calibers and larger for a dedicated bear gun.

Sighting-In Made Simple

Five simple steps to long-range accuracy

This is the Golden Age of the rifle. Never before have good rifles and rifle scopes been so affordable and accessible. Today's optics are far superior to the glass we used 20 years ago and a scope can be tailor made for an individual to wring astonishing accuracy from his or her rifle. A hunter can buy premium off-the-shelf ammo that, under the right conditions, is capable of minute-of-angle accuracy.

But all the advancements in manufacturing are no substitute for time at the shooting bench. Rifle, optics and cartridge have to be harnessed in a pre-hunt ritual we call sighting-in.

BORE-SIGHTING ISN'T GOOD ENOUGH At the sporting goods counter, a hunter can have his new scope bore-sighted by the same fellow who sold it to him. The technician uses his eye or a laser to align the scope with the bore. Bore-sighting saves a little time at the range, but it is no substitute for sighting-in. A bore-sighted rifle will probably be 'close,' but close might mean that the bullet strikes within three feet of point-of-aim at a hundred yards. That's not good enough when a big buck stands up across the canyon or a bull elk steps into a clearing 200 yards away.

Most rifle scopes have two turrets – one for windage (to move the bullet impact left or right) and one for elevation (to move impact up or down). Remove the turret caps and the crosshair can be adjusted by inserting a coin or twisting the dial clockwise or counter-clockwise. Most scopes are calibrated such that one 'click' equals an adjustment of 1/4-inch at 100 yards.

ALL AMMO IS NOT CREATED EQUAL

Sight-in with the ammunition you'll take on the hunt. Don't bring bargain-basement bullets to the range when you plan to use premium projectiles in the field. Downrange performance is likely to be very different. You can use the cheap stuff in practice if you want, but to establish accuracy, you want to use the hunting bullet.

And one box of 20 rounds is not sufficient. Take at least two boxes to the range and have another set aside for the hunt. If you're buying factory ammo, make sure the lot numbers match.

This revolver is fitted with custom grips to steady the gun in the hand for longer shots.

Scoped rimfire handguns, like this Ruger Charger, are at home in the alfalfa fields of eastern Oregon.

A .22 semi-automatic is a great camp gun and a backup to draw on a rabbit hunt. A scope makes a .22LR accurate on longer shots.

Here are five simple steps to take to make sure that your rifle is sighted-in before deer season.

1. Bore-sight it. Set the gun in a vise or bed it on sandbags. Point the muzzle in a safe direction. Remove the bolt and peer through the bore at a target and adjust the scope settings left or right and up or down to bring the crosshair into line with the bore. A laser bore-sighter may be used to good effect during this step. Just remember to remove the device before inserting ammunition.

2. Dry-fire it. Make sure the barrel is free of obstructions and pointed in a safe direction. Replace the bolt, set the safety and practice mounting the rifle to the shoulder. Flick the safety from 'safe' to 'fire' and, using the pad of the index finger, take the slack out of the trigger.

Have a partner watch to make sure the trigger finger is not transmitting flinch to the end of the barrel. When you're comfortable with the trigger and flinch is not an

issue, put the gun on the bench.

Note: Centerfire rifles are not damaged by dry-firing. And dry-firing is good practice. It helps the shooter gain familiarity with safety and trigger without burning expensive ammo. Don't dry-fire a rimfire, shotgun or a muzzleloader.

3) Bench-rest it. Create a solid rest for the gun from sandbags or use a bipod (only use a bipod if you plan to hunt with a bipod). Settle in behind the gun, snug it against your shoulder and settle your cheek on the stock. Don't grip the fore-end. That's what the bipod or the sandbags are for. Use the off-hand to stabilize the stock.

4) Establish the 25-yard zero. Set a target at 25 yards and fire three rounds to establish a group. Adjust the crosshair to center the group around the bulls-eye. This may take several adjustments and most of a box of ammo.

5) Tune the 100-yard group. After establishing a 25-yard zero, set a target at 100 yards and fire three rounds to establish a group. Depending on your hunting style, you may want your 100-yard group to impact three inches above the bulls-eye for a zero closer to 300 yards. Fine-tune the zero from the bench then replace the scope turret caps. The gun is sighted-in.

Now it's time to practice. Shoot off-hand, from improvised rests, from sitting, kneeling and prone positions. Use a bipod and shoot from shooting sticks. Shoot at close range and out to 300 yards and beyond.

This is the Golden Age of your rifle. Learn how to make it perform and your seasons will be golden.

Where to zero your big game rifle

One year, I used a Ruger .30-06 with a hand-loaded 165-grain Nosler AccuBond to take seven big game animals from antelope to elk with shots that ranged between 40 yards (Polynesian boar on Hawaii's Big Island) and 317 yards (pronghorn in Wyoming). I used a 100-yard zero and calculated bullet drop in minutes-of-angle with the Advanced Reticle Technology (www.hollandguns.com) in a Leupold rifle scope.

To zero my daughter's CZ550 (also chambered in .30-06), we used a different approach. This rifle was topped with an Alpen Apex sighted in for 250-yards. The bullet impacts on the bulls-eye at 25 yards and 250 yards. At 100 yards, it impacts at almost three inches above the bull. At 200 yards, it impacts at almost two inches above the bull. At 280 yards, the bullet will impact three inches low, still within the (six-inch) vital zone, without adjusting point-of-aim. If she has to take a 300 yard shot, the bullet will impact five inches low and requires a slightly higher hold.

This is the approach that, I think, works best for most hunters. To achieve a 250-yard zero, sight-in for a bullet impact of 2.75 to three inches above the bull at 100 yards.

BOW HUNTING

Archery tackle is highly personal equipment. What works well for one hunter will not work at all for another. Differences in stature, strength and preferences make each bow setup unique to the individual who put it together. For this reason, the hunter new to archery should listen to the advice of veteran archers but make their decisions based on their own personal preferences.

COMPOUND OR TRADITIONAL? Most archers use compound bows. The advantage is the draw weight let-off used to hold the bow at full draw. A longbow or a recurve takes 60 pounds to hold at draw length, but a compound bow set at the same weight may only require 21 pounds to keep it at full draw. Another advantage of the compound is the ease with which it can be accessorized. With bolt-on components, the compound bow is easily fitted with sights, a quiver, a rest, a string peep sight, a stabilizer and recoil reducers. Today, most compound shooters prefer to use a trigger-actuated release for consistency. The technology has allowed archers to shoot faster with better accuracy than ever before.

Some compound shooters have switched back to traditional equipment to experience what they call a purer form of archery. Longbows are the most difficult to shoot well. Recurves, with their double-flexed limbs deliver more energy to the arrow and less shock to the shooter's forearm.

Gary Lewis with a recurve on an elk hunt high in the mountains of northeast Oregon.

Technological or traditional, the best place to start is at an archery store. The dealer will let you try a bow to determine draw length and then assess your physical strength to decide how heavy a bow you can pull.

THE ARROW AND BROADHEAD The arrow is the most important piece of the archer's tackle. It must deliver the energy of the bow in a consistent manner, shot after shot, with the broadhead flying straight and true. To accomplish this, the arrow is spined for flex and is matched to the archer's draw length. Fletching may be either feather or plastic. Most compound shooters prefer plastic vanes, but feathered fletching shoots better through some rests.

For big game, a heavier arrow is preferred to carry the energy and the broadhead through the animal. With an arrow, the animal is killed not by shock as with a bullet, but by hemorrhage. That leads us to the broadhead. It should be the same weight as the practice field tip and it should be constructed to break bone with the tip and slice through hair, skin and organs with its razor sharp blades.

For an archer, the best shot to take is when the animal stands broadside or slightly quartering away. The arrow should be directed right behind the shoulder into the vital heart/lung area.

When you buy a new bow, take a few lessons. Consistency is the most important part of the routine to ensure that muscles are properly trained for the draw, the hold and the release. Your archery store may have a shooting range or, better yet, you can set one up in your own backyard. Shooting every day at known distances will help you to understand your limitations and enable you to judge distances accurately.

Scott Haugen glasses at last light in the desert east of Burns.

Take shots from a kneeling position as well as standing. Shoot uphill and downhill to learn how you and your equipment perform under a variety of conditions. Practice while wearing the same clothes that you will be hunting in. Will you wear gloves or a head net while hunting? Your shot will change if you put these on for the first time on opening day instead of practicing with them on in the preseason.

When hunting from a tree stand, the higher above the ground the stand is positioned, the steeper the angle of the shot. The steeper the angle, the trickier the shot for the archer, because a bear's spine protects the vitals. A better shot is made from the ground or just off the ground to allow the arrow to penetrate both lungs.

Informal "stump shoots' and organized events, like the popular 3-D courses, will polish your shooting skills and help you make those little adjustments in equipment and technique that can mean the difference between putting venison in the stew pot or buying the neat little shrink-wrapped packages at the store. ■

MUZZLELOADERS

In Oregon, hunters who choose the muzzle-loading rifle as a hunting tool have the opportunity to take advantage of special controlled hunts. Some of these hunts give the hunter a more liberal bag limit, allowing the taking of deer, antelope or elk of either sex.

Squirrels, rabbits and other small game may be hunted with any gun but a .36-.45 caliber might be

Rub an antler on a tree limb, tickle the tines, build the intensity. Deer sounds can bring other bucks and does in for a look.

In October, big blacktails often go nocturnal. But the cool of November and the scent of hot does sparks behavior that opens chinks in a blacktail's defenses.

the best choice. For big gamer, most hunters opt for a caliber of .50 or more.

The type of bullet you use should determine the rifling of the barrel. Some guns are set up to shoot patched round balls. These rifles have a slower rate of twist to stabilize the flight of the ball. A typical twist rate would be 1 turn in 66 inches. Also, the rifling is cut deeper to accommodate the patch.

If you will be shooting pre-lubed conical bullets a faster rate of twist, like 1 in 48, is optimum. These rifles will have shallower rifling.

If you are buying a gun to carry up the long hills and through brush and tall timber you might want to consider the maneuverability of the weapon. A long barrel adds weight to a gun but a shorter barrel doesn't allow the powder charge to develop as much energy.

A muzzleloading rifle is loaded by pouring a measured charge of powder down the barrel, then by seating a lubed patch and ball or a conical bullet on top of the charge.

With a flintlock gun the flint strikes steel to send a spark into a powder charge to ignite the powder in the barrel. A percussion or caplock gun fires a percussion cap that ignites the powder charge.

The lure of the blackpowder hunt lies in the solitary nature of the chase. And in the challenge of using a primitive weapon, stalking close and making one shot, your only chance, count.

With a 1-in-48 twist, the sidelock rifle prefers a diet of 100 grains of Hodgdon Triple 7, a lubed patch and a 320-grain pre-lubed lead conical bullet. A No. 11 cap provides the spark.

OREGON'S MUZZLELOADER RULES

In any hunt series with a season designation ending in "M" and certain 600 series hunts, the firearm must conform to the following standard as described in the Oregon Big Game Regulations:

"Muzzleloader" is any single-barreled (double barreled shotguns are permissible) long gun meant to be fired from the shoulder and loaded from the muzzle with an open ignition system (cap or flint exposed to the elements) and open or peep sights. Open ignition in-line percussion, sidelock under-hammer, top-hammer, mule ear percussion flintlock and wheellock guns are allowed.

During any hunt series with a season designation ending in "M" and certain 600 series hunts, the following rules apply to muzzleloader ammunition and loading:

It is illegal to hunt with jacketed bullets, sabots and bullets with plastic or synthetic bases. It is illegal to hunt with pelletized powders. It is illegal to hunt with centerfire primers as the ignition source. It is illegal to use scopes, but fiber optics and fluorescent paint incorporated into or on open or iron sights are legal.

SHOTGUNS & WINGSHOOTING

The shotgun is the most versatile tool a hunter can own. With the right shotgun a hunter can take everything from doves and squirrels to black bear and deer. But there are many different types of shotguns and different gauges and some shotguns are specialized for certain situations.

Up in the rimrock, Justin Silence swings on a chukar.

A 10 gauge gun is the biggest shotgun legal for hunting birds in Oregon. The next size down is a 12 gauge. This is the most common and versatile size of shotgun for all types of game. There is a 16 gauge, a 20 and a 28 as well as a shotgun called a four-ten, because the bore is measured at .410. A few other sizes of shotguns can be found but these are the most common.

Scott Linden, hunting quail and chukar in the snow.

Follow these guidelines when selecting your shotgun. For hunting big-game and taking long shots at goose or turkey, a 10 gauge will do the job when loaded properly. The 12 gauge is suitable for everything from upland birds to blacktail bucks. The same is true of the 16 and 20 gauge, though the bigger bore of the 12 allows for more pellets to be fired. The .410 is best suited for smaller game like squirrels, rabbits and doves.

Oregon hunters are allowed to carry no more than three rounds in their shotguns while hunting.

Choke on a shotgun refers to the amount that the shot string is constricted as it leaves the barrel. A full choke gun is better for shooting at longer distances, while a cylinder choke scatters the shot at closer range. Choke options are as follows: Cylinder (skeet), Improved Cylinder, Modified, Improved Modified and Full.

The right shotgun for a hunter will come to the shoulder easily, allowing the shooter to bring his or her eye in line with the barrel quickly and naturally. The fit of the gun to the shooter and its natural balance will make the difference between consistently hitting the target and missing it.

Don't take your new gun to the field until you have taken it to the practice range. You need to know the effective range of your weapon and the way it patterns at different distances and with different loads.

Time for a reload.

The first step is to trace a target roughly the size of the game you will be pursuing on a large piece of cardboard. If you will be hunting turkeys, trace a gobbler's vital area, the head and neck, on your target. If you will be hunting ducks, quail, doves or rabbits, sketch them out and set the target out at twenty yards. Mount the gun to your shoulder, sight along the barrel and fire. You should hit the target with a large percentage of pellets in the vital area of the target. A shotgun used mainly for upland birds should pattern slightly above the target to compensate for flushing birds.

Gene Adams calls for a clay on the course at Highland Hills Ranch.

Repeat the exercise at 30, 40 and 50 yards. You have exceeded your gun's effective range when there are few pellets striking the sketched image on your target.

If you are new to shotguns and wingshooting, take a lesson or a series of lessons at a local trap club or a sporting clays course. Try them going away until you can break them with regularity, then shoot them as they break to the left and right and as they tower or race along the ground. Practice translates to proficiency in the field.

Tuning up for the season.

OPTICS

BINOCULARS

For light transmission, field of view and portability in the field, the best binocular for the bear hunter is a porro prism model with a 7x or 8x magnification and 35mm to 50mm objective lens. These provide a wider field of view than roof prism models. Large, multi-coated objective lenses provide superior light-transmission. You may spend hours behind the glasses, watching for animals on the opposite hillside. Compacts just don't give the resolution, clarity, and ability to see in low light that full-size models provide.

A shoulder harness makes carrying binoculars a breeze.

Many hunters handicap themselves by carrying their binoculars in their backpacks. Binoculars should be quickly accessible. To minimize back and neck strain, use a strap system that puts the weight on the shoulders.

SPOTTING SCOPES

Sometimes it takes a closer look to pick an animal out of its habitat at long range. A spotting scope or a high-power binocular is one of the best investments a big game hunter can make. A

John Nosler behind the rifle at the COSSA Range east of Bend. Anticipated recoil translates to flinch. When sighting in, or in practice, use ear protection and watch your groups tighten.

spotting scope should give the hunter an option to examine the country at 15X and adjust to 35X or better for a zoomed-in view.

Buy the best spotting scope you can afford, because you will spend a lot of time using it. Low quality glass can give a hunter a headache and may reduce the time you can spend searching. If possible, take your top three choices outside of the store and

In canyon country, use binoculars to spot for game in each new fold of country.

A spotting scope can help a hunter pick deer out of the foliage out to a half-mile and beyond.

focus each in turn on some small distant object like a sign. Whichever scope renders the subject with the most clarity and color is the scope to choose.

In the field, you may have the opportunity to look at several animals before finding the one you are looking for. A spotting scope can make the

EQUIPMENT - OPTICS

When you spot an animal, watch it to determine whether it is likely to remain in the same area long enough to make a stalk.

difference on an open-country mule deer, pronghorn or spring bear hunt, but they may also be used in timbered country on the wet side of the mountains to probe small openings and edges.

Before beginning the stalk, plot a path that takes you into the wind, but keeps you behind hills, trees and other obstacles.

LASER RANGEFINDERS

For the big game hunter, one of the best optics developments is the laser rangefinder. On a hunt in unfamiliar terrain it is very difficult to estimate range with any degree of reliability. The best that two hunters could do before the rangefinder came along was for each to estimate the distance, compare estimates and then agree on a number in between. With a rangefinder, the guesswork is gone. All that remains is for the hunter to know the ballistics of his rifle and cartridge combination.

Some rangefinders are integral with binoculars. Most are a monocular that functions without readout until activated by depressing the trigger button one time. It is ready to 'shoot' the range when the display lights up in the viewfinder. Simply align the aperture on the target and press the button again.

Since this segment of the market is so new, the technology is current and all the major brands have high quality offerings. Some models have longer-range capability. Match the rangefinder to the real estate where you hunt. Decide what you can afford and compare several models side by side.

RIFLE SCOPES

A riflescope should be rugged enough to take the kind of abuse that can happen in rough, rocky country. It should not be prone to fogging. Spring storms can bring enough rain to fog cheaper optics. Make sure the riflescope is waterproof.

On a short-range rifle like a 30-30 or a 45-70, a two-power scope is a good choice. Shots will be at close range and the wide field of view afforded by the low power scope will allow the hunter to find the target quickly.

For longer range, the four-power is adequate for shots out to 300 yards. The four-power is simple. With it, there is never the chance that the scope will be set on a higher magnification when the shot must be taken at close range.

The problem with using higher power in

Hunting with a bipod? Sight-in with a bipod. Anytime changes are made to the rifle, scope, ammo or the shooting style, head to the range for another sight-in session to fine-tune accuracy at long range.

your scope is that it reduces the field of view. Field of view is the expanse of the subject within the field of the optical circle. As magnification is increased, the field of view diminishes. I have talked to many hunters who, when given a close range opportunity could not find the animal in the scope they had left dialed in at the maximum power. It is easier to find the target quickly in the scope when field of view is larger.

Reticles vary from a simple post with an aiming dot to military style mil-dots allowing the scope to be used as a range-finder. Plain crosshairs are fine but a duplex style crosshair is my choice on a hunting scope because the outer portion of each crosshair is very thick, tapering to a thin, aiming intersection. This configuration allows your eye to go quickly to the center of the scope.

The most important light transmitting feature is the size of the objective lens. The cone of light projected from the rear of the scope should

For his hunt in the White River canyon, James Flaherty put the data for his rifle/load combo inside the flip-up cap on his scope cover.

coincide with the diameter of the eye's pupil at low light. This is measured by arriving at the exit pupil. It should be between 5mm and 7mm. This is computed by dividing the objective diameter by the scope's magnification. So a 32mm objective with 4x magnification has an exit pupil of 8. A 40mm objective with 8x magnification has an exit pupil of 5.

Be more concerned with lens quality than lens size. Good optics will have coated lenses. The coating reduces reflection and enhances the passage of light, improving the clarity of what the hunter can see through the scope.

Choose the scope that is best for the type of hunting you intend to use it for and use the best quality rings and mounts to make it a part of your rifle. And spend whatever time and ammunition it takes to learn how the rifle/scope/cartridge combination performs at different distances.

STILL-HUNTING

Technology has turned man, the ultimate predator, into man, the consumer. We consume power, petroleum, potato chips, polyester, and prescriptions. We run around in circles, from home to school to job to grocery store and home again in the relentless pursuit of more goods to consume. Every year we get better at it, whirling faster and faster in our circles.

It's better to hunt several hundred yards of good cover well than to walk a dozen miles a day.

It is easy to bring our lifestyle to the woods and deserts, but it is not welcome there. In fact, it is counter-productive if the goal is to tie a tag on a deer. To succeed, we must become predators again.

Have you ever noticed how a deer can stand, rooted in one place for ten minutes or longer, while he processes information brought to him on the wind? Practice standing still for ten minutes the next time you walk in deer habitat.

Move as slow as a feeding deer. Take a step. Pause and look around, moving your eyes first. Watch for movement. Test the air with your nose. Sometimes you can smell the animal before you see him.

Wait 30 seconds or a minute or two. Then take another step and scan the woods from this new vantage. You are seeing a new view of the world framed in a different series of trees, looking for the horizontal line of a deer's back or the crook of a leg against the vertical world of trees and brush.

No other animal sounds like a human in the woods. Step, step, step, step, step. Deer don't move like that, squirrels don't move like that. Coyotes don't move like that. Only humans do. Don't let the cadence of your footsteps give you away.

Move slower than you ever imagined you could. Expect to see a deer. In good habitat, you will see them. If you move careful and cautious, you will see them before they see you.

When still-hunting, never take more than two steps. Any step you take without thoroughly scanning the terrain first, is a give-away move to the deer.

As long as the deer don't smell you first, they are counting on their hearing and vision to protect them. Hunt into the wind and keep your movement to a minimum. Face and hands are giveaways. Keep movement of hands to a minimum. When bowhunting, wear camouflaged gloves and face paint or head net.

Deer spot movement instantly. This ability to spot quick movement is what keeps them alive. Motionless, you can watch deer unobserved. Make a quick movement and you are sending the alarm that a predator is near.

Take light steps that test the ground before you put your weight down. Glance at the patch of trail ahead and subconsciously chart your path. Let the sole of your foot feel for a stick that might snap or gravel that might grind or dry leaves that might crunch. Still hunters should wear shoes or boots with a light sole that allow the hunter to detect noisemakers before they alert game.

Go slow. Move from cover to cover. If you have to get to the other side of a wide-open clearing, find a way around it, even if it means a detour. Your target animal

Still-hunting allows a hunter to set up for a call scenarioi.

might not see you cross the opening, but other animals will. The presence of a predator will make non-target animals more wary and their attitudes will be picked up by the deer. You can't afford to let this happen. You may have done everything else right. Don't take the easy, wide-open route if it will blow everything you have worked for to this point.

Spend extra time watching from the shade of a boulder or a tree. Keep your face and binoculars in the shade.

Binoculars are the second most important tool that the still-hunter carries. Don't leave them in the truck. Don't leave them in your pack. They do the most good when you are using them. If you are still-hunting you will use them often.

Still-hunting is solo sport. It is hard enough for one person to do well. However, two still-hunters can hunt a strip of timber separately, working into the wind. If one hunter bumps a deer, it may sneak toward his quieter partner.

Successful still-hunting is as much about attitude as it is about stealth. Believe that the slower you move, the more deer you will see.

KEEP THE WIND IN YOUR FAVOR Wind can be your ally or your biggest enemy. Your scent is frightening to most deer. They don't understand it, it signals danger to them. A deer's ability to smell is the one sense that they never question. The better you understand how deer react to dangerous odors, the better you will be able to exploit a deer's sense of smell.

If the wind is steady from one direction, hunt into it. A steady wind is the friend of the still-hunter. I carry and use a product called Smoke-In-A-Bottle. It is a white powder in a squeeze bottle. Squirted in the air, it allows the hunter to read wind direction. I rely on it, checking the wind constantly to make sure that the deer I am hunting won't catch my scent.

Don't fool yourself into believing that a deer might not smell you. If the wind is at your back the deer know you're there and you have severely limited your chance of success.

When scouting or hunting, watch where you walk and what you brush up against. Your scent will transfer to the brush, leaving a faint, lingering smell that warns animals of your presence long after you are gone.

When you choose your stand locations, pick a spot to take advantage of the prevailing wind and pick an alternate for those days when the wind is coming from the other direction.

If the wind appears to be swirling, it is better to back out of the hunt area and try another tactic rather than risk blowing a well-scouted location by spooking the animals out of it.

There are times when you can use scent to advantage. Hunting bedding areas, if you have good visibility, your scent can act as a driver, pushing deer out ahead. This tactic has saved the day for many hunters over the years.

Bryan Murphy checks the wind on a spring bear hunt in the Snake River Unit.

HUNTER SAFETY

Fall brings fog to the mountain valleys and a new chill to the morning air. Wisps of wood smoke whisper of coming winter. The leaves are changing color and the nights are getting long.

People feel an urgency to go and do. Fishermen, hikers and mountain bikers will take to the woods for a few more outings before snow flies. Bird, bear and bow hunters have been in the woods since August. With the coming of rifle deer season in October, many more hunters will be in the forests and mountains of our state.

There has been a steady decline in hunting accidents over the years, due in large part to a comprehensive hunter education program.

Youth bird hunts are a good way to introduce youngsters in a controlled environment, set up for success.

Hunter orange is recommended for anyone engaged in outdoor activities during the months of September through December.

There are a number of things you can do to lessen the risk of an accident: Avoid areas with high concentrations of hunters. Know which seasons are in effect for the area where you are hunting. During rifle and bird seasons wear hunter orange or other high visibility colors and avoid colors such as brown or white that other hunters might mistake for game.

Turkey hunters wear camouflage and call, imitating turkeys, from concealment. Never shoot unless you are sure of your target. Avoid wearing colors that might be mistaken for a turkey. Examine your gear as well. Are your arrows fletched with blue, red or white? These are the colors of a turkey's head. If you are using decoys, don't set up where another hunter may mistake your turkey for the real thing and shoot it and you.

Hunting with a party of other hunters presents more safety challenges. For several reasons, it is important that all members of your group know where each one is likely to hunt. If one hunter doesn't return to camp at the end of the day then the others will know in which direction to search.

Insist that other members of your party wear high visibility clothing. An orange cap or a vest makes it easy to identify a fellow hunter in low light situations.

Hunter orange keeps everyone safer on a bird hunt.

When hunting together in places where you may be separated by brush, have your companions wear an orange or red hat. If game flushes you want to be certain where your friend is before you shoot. Never shoot over the head of another person. There is no trophy bird, rabbit, deer or elk that is more important than a human life.

Watch other hunters carefully. Careless muzzle control can kill. When a firearm is passed from one person to another, the gun should be disabled. Set the safety mechanism to the 'SAFE' position, open the bolt on a rifle, or the action of a shotgun before crossing a fence, fording a stream or climbing a cliff.

Check the shotgun to make sure it is empty before putting it away at the end of the day.

Always unload your firearm before putting it in a boat, a pickup or any other vehicle. Never put the gun in a case while it is still loaded. Never grasp the barrel of a gun to pull it toward you. Never

DAY SEMINARS

3 STATION ROTATION OF:

1. Five Stand

Sporting Clays
5 Stand is a form of Sporting Clays with a wide variety of targets being thrown to simulate field shooting.

2. Live

Pheasant Hunt
This is an opportunity for the participants to participate in a live pheasant hunt with a guide and trained dogs. After the hunt they learn how to harvest their birds.

3. Introduction to

Fly Fishing
Learn the working parts of a fly rod and basic casting skills.

FIREARM SAFETY
Upon arrival you and your child are introduced to our instructors and given instruction on the fundamental rules for safe gun handling.

ADVANCED DAY SEMINARS ARE AVAILABLE

HUNTER SAFETY CAMP

State Certified hunter safety course.

"I sent you a boy and received a young man back. I now have a hunting buddy for life..."

"I didn't have any favorites because I loved it all..."

"If you want your child to learn about hunting and safety, you could not find a better place to give your child the chance to find themselves other than YOA."

Jeff & Jenn DuPont

Grass Valley, OR

Resv: **541.390.0285**
Info: **541.350.4197**
Fax: **541.475.3757**

put yourself in a position where the barrel of your gun or someone else's gun is pointing at you. Never let anyone else swing the muzzle of their gun carelessly in your direction.

There is no place for alcohol on a hunt. With firearms, friends and family around, the stakes are just too high to take the risk of impaired judgment.

If you will be hunting alone, don't take unnecessary risks; always tell a friend where you are going and when you will return. If you don't return on time or in a reasonable amount of time then someone will come looking.

At the end of a successful hunt, unload your weapon. Don't pack your trophy out until you have tied hunter-orange ribbons to the head and body.

A spare tire, chains and a jack. You're going to need them eventually.

Even a logger who knows the road can put it in the ditch once in a while.

HUNTING GEAR AND SURVIVAL SKILLS

MAP AND COMPASS

It doesn't take long to get turned around when there are no landmarks. And relying on your own internal compass is a good way to get farther off course.

All travel requires some type of navigation. Start by spending time at home, poring over maps of the hunt area. Try to picture the lay of the land by picking out landmarks.

Navigating in the backwoods is easy to learn and usually does not have to be precise. However, in the event of an emergency involving a member of your party, you must be able to find your way out by the quickest route possible, describe the situation to a rescue team, pinpoint the exact location and be able to direct or lead help back to your injured partner.

Most people are not intimately familiar with the places they hike, hunt or fish. But you don't need to be to find your way from one spot to another and back again. You just need to follow a few simple rules.

Bring a good compass. It doesn't need to be expensive but it should be reliable and of the protractor type with a dial that can be rotated 360 degrees.

Carry maps of the hunt area with you. Use your compass when you leave camp. Note direction of travel and refer back to your compass when you change course.

Try this exercise. Stand holding your compass and note in which direction the magnetic needle points. This is magnetic north. Orient your map so that the north arrow points in the same direction as the compass needle.

Place the compass on the paper with the edge of the instrument along the intended line of travel. Then turn the dial until 'N' points to north. Note that direction in degrees is read at the index line of the dial.

Declination is the difference between magnetic north and true north. Make the adjustment recommended on the map for the area you are in. Compensate for declination by rotating the dial the distance indicated on the map legend.

Next, pick up the compass and hold it level so that the needle is free to rotate. Turn your body until the pointing end of the needle aligns with the orienting arrow and 'N' on the dial. Sight along the direction of travel indicator and pick out a distant landmark, whether it be a tree, a rock or a mountain. Proceed to your landmark and pick out a new one from there. Follow this pattern until you arrive at your destination.

GPS

A Global Positioning System receives and interprets signals from satellites in orbit above the earth. At any time, at almost any place, a handheld GPS unit can tell you exactly where you are. Of course, if you're already lost when you consult your GPS for the first time you won't benefit too much from having a machine confirm it. But if you, prior to getting lost, establish a point to return to, then

Trip Planning Checklist

Directional wind indicator
Cover scent
Binoculars
Spotting scope
Laser range finder
Knife
Back-up knife
Whetstone
Rifle
20-rounds ammunition
Calls
Survival gear
Unit or county maps
Topographic maps
Compass
Global Positioning System (GPS) unit
Rope
Come-along or winch
T-Hanger and tackle for skinning
Game bags
Camera
Surveyor's tape
Canteen
Extra batteries for all electronics

Topo maps can provide the clues to help you find unpressured bucks or bulls. And a working knowledge of map and compass can save your life.

you can easily use the instrument to find your way back.

The Global Positioning System was originally developed for the U.S. Department of Defense as a highly accurate navigational and targeting system. They lock on to high-frequency radio signals from some of the satellites in orbit and calculate through triangulation the exact location of the hand-held unit.

At any time, a hunter can set and mark points along the path that he might want to return to. Once, on a deer hunt, I found a spring burbling clean cold water. I marked it as a waypoint on my GPS. After

A GPS unit is a great tool for scouting and for finding your way in and out of unfamiliar country. But it is no substitute for a knowledge of a map and compass. And you'd better bring extra batteries.

we killed and packed out a big buck that day, we were able to, with confidence, find that spring again and refresh ourselves before walking out to the truck.

A GPS unit is much more than just a high-priced

Survival Fanny Pack Checklist

- Space Blanket
- Waterproof matches
- Cigarette lighter
- Compass
- Map
- GPS
- Extra batteries
- Flashlight
- Fire starter
- Energy bar
- Parachute cord
- Surveyor's flagging
- Rubber gloves
- Water bottle

compass. For instance, a hunter pining away for snow to melt can sit at his dinner table and plot out the latitude and longitude of a high mountain meadow he wants to scout. By entering the coordinates into the GPS unit, he can hike straight to it in the spring just by following a course set months earlier in the comfort of his home.

Similarly, a bowhunter scouting in mid-summer, can pinpoint the meadow where he wants to be on opening day. Instead of stringing orange flagging all over a mountain to follow back in before the sun comes up, he can just return to the original waypoint using the backlit screen to show the way.

A friend once told me of the time when, after much scouting, he found a meadow loaded with elk sign. It was definitely the place he wanted to be when the season opened. Setting a waypoint, he returned to his truck and started driving roads, watching the digital readout until he found the spot where he could park closest to the meadow. On opening day he was back there with just a minimum of effort.

It should be stressed, however, that a GPS won't get you out of the woods when your only set of batteries dies. And satellite contact can be lost in

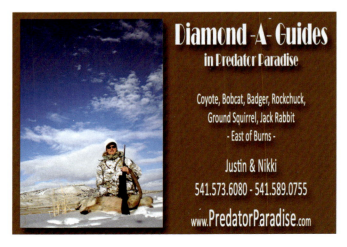

dense cover and deep canyons. Be sure to have extra batteries and a good map and compass for a backup

SURVIVAL

How to Build a Shelter

Sometimes there is no alternative to spending a night in the woods. In most cases, you won't have a sleeping bag with you, or a tent. You have to make do with what you have in your survival pack or day pack. When you determine that there is no way

A fire can be a big morale boost on a wet, cold elk hunt. Carry at least two different ignition sources and dry tinder when going into elk country.

that you can find your route out before dark, and if you are too far into the woods to make it out safely, resign yourself to roughing it and make camp before nightfall.

You can do without food, you can do without water, but you must have shelter to keep from growing hypothermic in the long, cold night ahead.

If you have a plastic tarp, a space blanket, or a poncho, you are ahead of the game. If you are without those items, you can still spend the night in reasonable warmth, if you keep your head and build a shelter.

The most important thing to do is stay calm. Millions of people over thousands of years, have spent unplanned nights outside and survived. So can you.

Pick a spot where you can find shelter from the prevailing wind: in the lee of a boulder, a fallen tree or a cliff. Using tree limbs, build two more walls in the shape of a lean-to to shelter you, your bed, and your fire from weather. Make a thatched roof of pine or fir boughs over your head. If you have a plastic tarp, lay boughs on top of it to keep out rain and snow.

Gather as much dry firewood as you can find. Get more than you think you will need. It may be necessary, in the middle of the night, to restart your fire. Keep a stack of dry wood close to hand.

Build your fire against a boulder, or a stack of logs. As much as possible, you want to direct the heat inside your shelter where it will do the most good.

Hollow out a depression in the ground for a bed. Line it with needles or leaves and stack a pile of boughs nearby. When your fire is burning bright and your day is done, you can pull the boughs over you and keep hypothermia at bay.

ODFW
Mandatory Reporting of Harvest and Effort

Don't forget to report! ODFW requires individuals with big game tags (except Bighorn Sheep and Rocky Mt Goat) and turkey tags to complete the Mandatory Reporting of Harvest and Effort survey. See Oregon Big Game Regulations or www.dfw.state.or.us for more details.

OREGON DEPARTMENT OF FISH AND WILDLIFE

SHED ANTLER HUNTING

Shed Antlers Provide Scouting Clues for Deer and Elk Hunters

Mule deer, blacktail deer and whitetails drop their antlers between January and March. Elk usually drop their headgear between March and May. Their castoff crowns can provide scouting clues for hunters hoping to tie their tags on older age-class bucks and bulls.

20 years ago, the pursuit of antlers was practiced by a few. These days it has become a passion that, for some people, replaces the hunt. Antlers are made into lamps, chandeliers, chairs, tables and lots of other things. Like any commodity, the price fluctuates. But a brown, top-quality fresh four-point chandelier-ready deer antler can bring $14 a pound, while a set of trophy-class antlers may bring thousands.

Some guys justify the cost of their ATVs with the money they bring home from the antler buyer.

Several outfitters have cashed in on the craze and are offering guided shed hunts. No hassles with transporting guns and bows in airports, but you'd better bring a good backpack and be ready to pay excess baggage fees on the way home.

Several shed organizations have sprung up. One of the better organized groups is the Oregon Shed Hunters (www.oregonshedhunters.com), based in Central Oregon. They put on group hunts, offer contests and keep records. The North American Shed Hunters Club (www.shedantlers.org) lists news about auctions and how to connect with collectors. A site dedicated to the training of antler dogs can be found at www.antlerdogs.com.

Steve Waller, the owner of Cabin Creek Kennels (www.cabincreekgundogs.com) in Oakland, Oregon, has been training dogs since 1971. He has been training antler dogs for the last six years.

"Labs work very well because they're a natural retriever," Waller said. "When the ground is wet and there is more undergrowth, a lab might be the best choice because they hunt with their heads down. A good upland dog hunts with its head up and he's going to smell a chukar; he'll also smell an antler."

"They need to have a strong desire to retrieve, probably stronger than normal. In a lot of cases, that antler has been laying there for a year." Which means the dog may not be quite as excited about finding a dried piece of deer headgear as he might get about jumping a chukar or covey of quail.

"The key thing is they need to be force-fetch trained so that once they get the antler in their mouth, they'll deliver it to hand," Waller said.

On spring and summer scouting trips, using a dog to locate sheds can save a lot of time and help a hunter focus. One hunter who tagged a record-class Roosevelt elk with his recurve bow last year, credited his success to his dog, who found the antlers first.

"No more than a handful of people are using antler dogs right now," Waller said. "A lot of these guys are terribly secretive." With good reason. They've figured out that man's best friend is not going to tell their buddies about the best hunting spots or beat them to the trophy when the season opens.

Brian Davis with a matched pair of elk sheds he found while walking the ridgetops.

Some breeds, like this pudelpointer, are easily trained to hunt for shed antlers.

TAXIDERMY

WILDFOWL TAXIDERMY

Some hunting memories can be preserved through taxidermy. As you look at that wood duck on the mantle in the years to come you will be transported back in time to the moment when the drake opened his wings and took to the air in an explosion of sound and a spray of water.

A good taxidermist can make him seem to come alive again. But you have to do your part in bringing that bird in from the field.

Select a bird for mounting on the basis of its plumage, the glossy sheen of its feathers and, possibly, its size. Pick one that has not been damaged by shot or a hard-mouthed retriever. Then try to handle the bird as little as possible. Do not gut the bird or draw it.

A bobcat and chukar mount by McLagan's Taxidermy.

Carry it by the feet with the head down so that any blood will drain off. If there is blood on the feathers, daub it with a wet tissue or cloth before it can dry and stain the feathers.

The next step is to take your trophy back to the car or leave it in a safe place. If in the car, don't seal the car up, allow for proper ventilation and don't leave the bird where the heat from the sun will go to work on it. Lay it on a clean piece of paper and make sure that tail feathers or wingtips are not bent.

Birds that will not be taken to the taxidermist immediately can be frozen. In the case of a bird with long tail feathers, lay the bird on a piece of cardboard, laying out the feathers so that you can wrap with clear freezer wrap, securing the bird to the board.

BIG GAME MEMORIES

One of the best ways to preserve the memory of a hunt is through taxidermy. Proper field care of the big game trophy can contribute immensely to the quality of the finished mount. Follow these rules after gutting the animal and cooling the meat:

Never make any cuts below the head, forward of the front legs. Do not cut the throat. Instead, skin down the back of the neck in a straight line, as near center as possible and then make a second cut forming a "Y" running to the base of the antlers. Cut carefully around the antlers by cutting the skin away from the base.

Go slow and careful with the next two steps. Cut the ear cartilage from the bone on the inside and clean the meat away from the base of the ear. Skin along the skull, careful not to cut through at the eyelids.

Cut the lips close to the skull, leaving the lips attached to the skin. Make the cut inside the lips.

Leave enough of the cape for a shoulder mount. Cut inside the front legs in order to include the brisket for a complete shoulder mount.

The top portion of the skull, the antlers and the bone between them, is all that is needed for mounting. Simply saw off the top of the skull through the center of the eyes after skinning is complete.

You will need approximately two pounds of non-iodized salt for a deer cape, approximately four pounds for an elk cape. Use your skinning knife to remove the extra meat from the hide and salt it heavily. Rub the salt into the scalp and leave it rolled up for a few hours in the shade. Then turn the skin flesh side out and salt it again.

Roll it up and let it drain some more.

Take the hide and antlers to a taxidermist as soon as possible or put them in the freezer wrapped in plastic.

EUROPEAN MOUNTS If you want a unique trophy that you can prepare yourself, consider making a European mount of your buck deer.

For a European mount, peel the skin over the head and nose. If special care is taken, the cape can be saved and sold or traded to a taxidermist.

Wear rubber gloves and eye protection for the following work.

With a hacksaw or similar tool, cut into the cranium, aiming for a spot just below the eyes. Discard lower jaw.

With a small, sharp knife, trim out the brains, and eyeballs. Cut the extra meat away from the skull and discard.

Outside, start water boiling in a big kettle and pour some salt into the water. Boil the skull, keeping the antlers out of the water. When the meat is thoroughly cooked, remove it from the water.

Clean all dirt from the antlers with water and a light bristle brush.

Next, trim the cartilage out of the nasal passages and chip away the dried meat from the various orifices on the skull.

Boil the skull again when all the meat and cartilage has been cut away. When withdrawing it from the water, pull it out fast to keep the fats on the surface from adhering to the skull again. Spray the skull quickly with water from a garden hose.

Next, mix a cup of bleach in with clean water in your kettle. Allow the skull to soak in the bleach for twenty minutes. Do not let antlers come into contact with bleach. Remove and spray clean with garden hose.

Allow skull to air dry. This may take from two days to two weeks, depending on the humidity.

When the skull is dry, spray antlers with clearcoat lacquer and allow to dry overnight.

Mask antlers and spray cleaned, bleached skull with flat white paint and allow to cure overnight.

The skull can then be hung on a plaque – a trophy that will give you pleasure for the hunt it reminds you of and the effort invested.

Greg Erickson, of Swiftcreek Elements with a set of reproduction mule deer antlers.

Bama's Wildlife Reflections

Bill Surber, Taxidermist
1804 Carlson Drive
Klamath Falls, OR 97603

541.778.2749
www.bwrtaxidermy.com

MEAT CARE

Bullet placement is the first consideration in the care of your game. Properly placed, a good bullet will down the animal quickly with little meat damage. Taking the time to know your quarry's anatomy before you hunt will pay off when it's time to take the shot. Taking the time to choose your target carefully will mean that as little damage as possible is done to the meat.

An animal on the ground doesn't mean that the hunt is over. In fact, the most critical phase of the process has just begun. The animal should be cleaned within the first ten to fifteen minutes after it goes down.

Working on a bear in the Imnaha country. It is important to remove the hide quickly in warm weather.

This doesn't have to be an unpleasant experience. A little preparation before the hunt goes a long way toward making this part easier. A novice should be carrying written, illustrated instructions to show the way.

In my pack, I carry a knife, a bone saw, about two feet of cord and surveyor's flagging to mark the trail back if I have to make more than one trip or go for help. In the truck I'll have a tarp and deer bags to protect the meat.

Some people prefer to skin the animal in the field. This may be a good idea if you will be packing it out on your back. Otherwise, you may want to leave the skin on to protect the meat while dragging it. Let the conditions dictate how you'll handle this. On a warm day, you may need to remove the skin to allow the meat to cool faster. Dragging the carcass to the truck or camp, leave the skin on to protect it from the ground. With the meat back in camp, skin and hang in the shade.

On the road home or to the butcher's there are a number of ways to keep the meat fresh. Displaying it on the hood of the truck is not one of them. Meat and heads tied on in such a manner are subject to spoilage by engine heat and exhaust and drying by the wind. And the practice is offensive to non-hunters. But don't hide it by piling luggage on top of the animal either, as this will insulate the meat against cooling. Allow for good movement of air and prop the cavity open to allow cool air to circulate. If you've already started butchering it yourself, chances are you can get most of it in a cooler.

Wild game meat is not only good tasting and good for you, it is an expression of our freedom and part of our heritage. Take the time before the hunt to

decide how you'll care for the meat, recognize how weather conditions and other factors play a part in spoilage. Wasting meat that could be saved is not only unethical, it is illegal. Properly cared for, deer and elk meat is some of the best tasting food you can get. You not only owe it to the animal, you owe it to yourself to take the best care of it you can.

INSTRUCTIONS FOR CLEANING DEER AND ANTELOPE

1. To clean a big game animal, you will need rubber gloves, (2) 18-inch lengths of cord and a knife.
2. Place the animal on its back, with the head uphill if possible.
3. Tie a cord around the penis to lessen the risk of urine tainting the meat.
4. Cut around the anus with your knife, then tie a cord around the end of the anus to keep excrement from the meat.
5. Cut from the pelvis bone up to the sternum, cutting around and laying aside the testicles or the udder on a doe. Take care not to nick the intestines with the tip of the blade.
6. With the animal's head uphill, the internal organs will sag. Reach into the cavity and cut away the diaphragm, holding the stomach out of the way with your other hand.
7. Reach into the cavity and grasp the windpipe and gullet, pulling toward you. Cut them off as far forward as possible.
8. Tip the carcass so the internal organs slide out. You may have to cut some tissue that is holding the organs.
9. Turn the animal belly-side down to let the cavity drain.
10. Remove the legs below the knees and hang carcass from the hocks. Clean and sharpen your knife before skinning the animal.

To be ready to deal with a big game animal, bring a sharp knife, a length of cord and game bags. Allow the meat to cool quickly.

The **OREGON TAG GUIDE** reveals the effect of Oregon's preference point system for issuing big-game tags. For each of Oregon's 600-plus limited-entry hunts, the specific chance of drawing a tag is forecasted for different preference points. Recent harvest success rates are provided. Discover the effects of making a 2nd choice, applying as a group, or being a non-resident. There is strategic advice for youths. Oregon's top Boone & Crockett Club entries are listed for all big-game species. Over 140 pages that include wildlife unit maps, sky tables, hunting camp checklist, binocular basics, and more. Use the **OREGON TAG GUIDE** and make an informed decision when selecting a controlled big-game hunt.

Tag guides are $14.95 each plus $7.95 per order for shipping and handling.

Phone orders (24 hrs): **1.800.266.1622**

Mail orders: **PERCENTAGE TAGS**
PO Box 3610
Salem, OR 97302

OUTFITTERS

GOING GUIDED

Outdoor shows are where many hunting guides book most of their new business for the year. You get there early on a Saturday, push your way through the crowd, look at the photos and soon imagine yourself still-hunting down some forest trail or glassing a juniper-studded slope for mule deer.

Will it be everything you imagined it to be? There are steps you can take to ensure that your trip across the state or across the country will be successful.

Decide first who you want to spend all that time with. What can you expect from your regular partners? Are they the kind of people who will keep their spirits up when the rain falls for four days straight and much of your time is spent trying to keep dry? You should only hunt with people with similar expectations.

Be equally careful with who you book. Ultimate success is not guaranteed. You are still subject to the same variables you experience closer to home. It could rain the whole time and blow out all the rivers, or an unseasonable snowstorm might drive the animals to lower elevations. Be careful if the outfitter assures you that you will bag your buck or your bull or your bear. Real life does not always work that way.

Too often, a well-polished smile, a colorful display, some trophies and a few full-color photos are enough to convince us to part from our money.

REFERRALS If the outfitter is worth the money, there will be a list of clients who have hunted with them. And there will be a list of folks who will give a good recommendation. Of course, those former clients should get a phone call, but the best referrals aren't on the list at all.

Ask for the names and contact information of the clients who went home empty-handed. Find out why, but remember there are two sides to every story. To be fair, some clients are simply not equipped for success, due to unrealistic expectations or other self-imposed limitations.

At the end of a successful hunt in northeast Oregon. *Photo courtesy Barry Cox*

Ask the reference about the guide's ethics. And ask if they would book a trip with that outfitter again.

Go on-line and find out what other hunters have to say. Organizations such as The Hunting Report, Safari Club International, and the North American Hunting Club, among others, keep files on outfitters.

Will it be everything you imagined it to be? You can be more confident if you ask the right questions in advance.

WHAT TO EXPECT Every hunt is different. Want to know what to expect? Ask all the questions beforehand.

License and tag fees are probably not included in the price of the hunt. Air travel from your home to the jumping-off point is probably not included, but the price of float plane travel may be. Find out in advance.

Meals are often included in the price of the hunt, but some outfitters have opted to exclude food as a way to keep prices down.

Ask the outfitter what you should expect of him and his crew and assure him what he can expect of you. Will you be expected to haul water, chop wood or feed the horses? How will the hunt be conducted? Does the guide use spot-and-stalk methods or will he put you on a stand in the morning and come pick you up again after dark? Will the guide butcher and pack out your animal?

Ask also about the previous year. A client has the right to know if a severe drought or a hard winter took a toll on wildlife.

Food can make or break the experience. If it's hard to live without a big breakfast or steak and seafood every night, let the outfitter know about it in advance. If money is tight, the cook might be forced to make sandwiches with bologna and processed cheese. If you can't stand that kind of fare, make sure the outfitter knows about it in advance. And if it's imperative that there be chocolate bars or a half-dozen cookies in the lunch sack, bring them yourself.

On the hunt, if there are support personnel involved, such as guides, cooks and deckhands, it doesn't hurt to tip a little in advance of the final gratuity. The crew can get burnt out toward the end of a long season and a little attitude adjustment in the form of some folding money, cheerful smiles and a charitable demeanor on your part will go a long way toward making the trip a good one.

WHAT THE GUIDE EXPECTS FROM THE CLIENT

The outfitter and guide want to see every hunt end with the client having had at least an opportunity to tag a bear. The reality of hunting is that not every hunter will do it right. An opportunity is all a client can reasonably expect.

The guide expects the hunter to have done at least a little bit of research about the animal and its tendencies, habits and habitat.

A guide's biggest disappointment is the client who didn't have the self-discipline in the months before the hunt to get in shape. I once watched a hunter stop a stalk when he was 150 yards from the bear because he just couldn't walk any farther. That bear walked away and the hunter never had another chance.

Lunch in the field might come in a sack, or it might be a four-course affair.

On a western spot-and-stalk hunt, there might be miles to cover on foot. The stalk might come in the last hour of light with a slope to descend and another to climb before a shot is made. And when the hunt is with hounds and the bear is treed, there may only be a few minutes to get from point A to point B before the bear decides to go mano-a-mano with the dogs.

Start walking or jogging at least three times a week. Go to the gym. Climb the stairs at work instead of taking the elevator. Get a personal trainer. Do whatever it takes, but lose the weight and gain the lung capacity to go that last 150 yards.

In my experience, most hunters go over-gunned. Make sure you can shoot whatever you bring and shoot it well. The best guides will require that you shoot first before they take you on a hunt. Be prepared or expect to be embarrassed if you can't put three bullets in a five-inch circle at a hundred yards.

Get in good physical shape and make sure you are bringing the right gear for the weather that might be encountered. Practice shooting under the conditions and at the distances you will encounter in the field. When you finally arrive at your destination, go at it with all the enthusiasm you can muster.

Be cheerful, stay out all day and listen to your guide. You paid him your hard-earned money to make your stay worthwhile. The attitude you take will help create the memories you bring home.

WILD GAME COOKING

ELK SLIDERS WITH CARAMELIZED ONION CHUTNEY AND ROGUE CREAMERY BLEU CHEESE

Small hamburger (slider) buns
2 pounds Ground Elk
Rogue Creamery Smoked Bleu Cheese
1 Red Onion finely chopped
1/2 cup Italian Parsley finely chopped
1 Tbsp Black Pepper
1 Tbsp Salt
1/2 cup Olive Oil
1/2 teaspoon dried Thyme
1/2 cup Sherry Vinegar
1 Tbsp Sugar

For the burger: mix onions, parsley, salt and pepper and ground elk. Form into little burger patties. Brush with olive oil and grill three minutes per side.

For the caramelized onions: take five red onions and slice thinly. Toss with half a cup of olive oil, half a teaspoon of dried thyme, tablespoon of sugar and half cup of good sherry vinegar. Toss the onions with the olive oil and the thyme then roast the onions on a half sheet pan in the oven at 400 degrees for ten minutes. Stir and roast for another ten minutes. Then put onions in a bowl and add the sherry vinegar and sugar. Allow to cool for a couple of hours. Add a little olive oil if consistency is too dry. Grill the elk burgers then top off with caramelized onions and add a thin slice of smoked Rogue Bleu Cheese on top and sandwich in mini slider buns.

"Goes well with a really good Oregon Pinot or a Walla Walla, WA Syrah."

Courtesy Chef Ramsey Hamdan-Joolz, Bend, OR

VENISON BULGOGI SANDWICHES – serves 4

600g Red Stag (or deer or elk) stir fry
8 Spring Onions
1 Tbsp Sesame Oil
White buttered Scottish Bab or Sesame Seed Bun
Garnish
Kim Chee (pickled cabbage)
Soy Sauce (for garnish)
Sesame Oil

Marinade

1/4 cup Sesame Seeds
1/3 cup light Soy Sauce
4 cloves Garlic
1 Tbsp grated Ginger
1 Tbsp Hoisin Sauce (optional)
1/4 cup Soybean Oil

A Korean recipe with New Zealand flair. Cut the venison into thin strips or use pre-prepared stir-fry venison. Toast the sesame seeds until lightly browned. Cool and grind into a fine powder with a coffee grinder. For the marinade, combine soy sauce, garlic, grated ginger and soybean oil and mix well. Use enough marinade to coat the venison stir-fry and stand for 15 minutes. Slice the spring onions. Heat a heavy pan, wok or flat top BBQ until very hot. Add a touch of sesame oil for cooking and stir-fry the marinated venison quickly for 1 minute. Add the onions and stir. Serve with steamed rice, a side dish of cabbage and a small bowl of light soy sauce and toasted sesame seeds.

Courtesy Sarah Burdon – Glen Dene Station – Lake Hawea, NZ

WILD TURKEY ON A PLANK

1 boneless Wild Turkey breast (approximately 1 pound)
2 Tbsp Dijon Mustard
2 Tbsp Rum
1 Tbsp Honey
1 Tbsp Canola or Olive Oil
1 teaspoon Coriander
1/2 teaspoon meat tenderizer (optional)
4-6 strips raw bacon
1 plank soaked in water, at least 30 minutes

Place turkey breast in a sealable plastic bag. In a small bowl mix all ingredients, except bacon. Pour marinade into bag with turkey. Marinate in refrigerator 2-24 hours. Soak

an alder, cedar or hickory plank 1-2 hours in water or apple juice. Dry plank 1-2 minutes in a hot grill or oven. Coat top of plank with a thin layer of olive or canola oil. Place turkey on plank. Cover turkey breast with sliced bacon. Grill on a medium-hot grill or bake at 375° 30-60 minutes or until meat thermometer reads 170°. Slice and serve directly off plank if desired.

To see this recipe prepared on video or for more wild turkey recipes, go to www.tiffanyhaugen.com

Cooking Tips:

* Do not overcook wild turkey, use a meat thermometer and cook only to 170°.
* Wild turkey is very lean, add fat by layering with bacon, sausage or baste frequently.
* When sliced thinly, wild turkey breast can be cooked quickly for stir fry or casseroles.
* Add extra olive oil when cooking ground turkey meat.
* After the turkey has been "breasted-out" use the rest of the bird to make excellent soups and stock.

"Wild turkey is an easy to attain, healthy and flavorful game meat. Planked, grilled, sauteed, ground or made into jerky, this versatile game lends itself to a variety of recipes."

Courtesy Tiffany Haugen, author. (www.tiffanyhaugen.com)

BACON WRAPPED STUFFED VENISON STEAK

4 Venison Steaks
Ground Pork Sausage
4 Bacon Strips
Onions
Peppers
Olive Oil

Start with hot sauté pan with a little olive oil. Saute onions and peppers till soft. Add ground pork sausage and sauté till browned. Put aside for later in bowl. Use pan to partially cook bacon strips for wrap. Using small sharp knfie, cut venison steak open like a pouch. Stuff pouch with sausage, peppers and onion mix and wrap with bacon strip. Use toothpick to hold together. Warm oven to 375 degrees. Sprinkle French fried onions over steak and bake in hot oven till steak is cooked medium rare (8 to 10 minutes depending on the cut). For my dinner, I make skin-on rough mashed garlic red potatoes with shredded cheddar cheese and asparagus with Hollandaise sauce. Enjoy!

Courtesy Outdoor Chef Kurt Ploetz – (www.fishgriller.com)

GROUSE AND SPINACH SAUTÉ - serves 2 or 3

2 Grouse (substitute quail, pheasants or chukar)
Fresh Spinach Leaves
1 large Tomato
1 small Sweet Onion
1 cup sliced Mushrooms
2 Tbsp Butter
Salt and Pepper to taste

Saute spinach, tomatc, onion and mushrooms in butter. Set aside. Brown each side of grouse in butter till clear juices flow. Add vegetable mixture over grouse and serve.

Courtesy Merrilee Lewis

SWEET CHILI GOOSE BREAST SAUTÉ OVER WILD RICE

4 Goose Breasts, filleted, cleaned (substitute duck)
Wild Rice
Red Peppers
Yellow Peppers
Sweet Onion
Butter
Tony Chachere's Creole Seasoning
Johnny's Seasoning
Montreal Steak Seasoning
Big Dan's Sweet Chili Sauce
1/2 cup Water

Begin with four filleted, cleaned and washed goose breasts. Slice in 1/8-inch strips across the grain. Start a big sauté pan with 1/2 stick of butter melting. In a boiler pot, start the rice cooking. Slice 1/4 cup each of red and yellow peppers. Fine dice a sweet onion in ¼-inch squares. Add minced garlic to sauté pan then add peppers and onion to soften and brown. Season with one teaspoon

each of Johnny's Seasoning, Montreal Steak Seasoning and Tony Chachere's Creole Seasoning. Pour in 1/2 cup Big Dan's Sweet Chili Sauce and then add goose breast slices.

Sauté till goose breast slices are done medium well. Add 1/2 cup water to make sauce then turn off and cover till rice is done. Place a bed of rice on each plate and then a generous portion of goose sauté on top. Add a large spoonful of juice on top of sauté and rice. Then sit down and enjoy.

Courtesy Outdoor Chef Kurt Ploetz – www.fishgriller.com

SALAMI

5 lb. Hamburger or Venison or Elk
4 Tbsp Curing Salt (Morton's Tender Quick)
2 1/2 Tsp Liquid Smoke
1 Tsp Garlic Salt
2 1/2 Tsp Coarse pepper or peppercorns
2 1/2 Tsp Mustard seed

Knead all ingredients together, put in a covered bowl and refrigerate. Every day for four days, knead for 5 minutes, cover and return to refrigerator. On the 4th day, knead for 5 minutes and form into 2 or 4 rolls as desired. Place on a rack over a cookie sheet to catch drippings and bake for 9 hours at 160 degrees. Cool and slice.

A few comments about the recipe: use plain hamburger. Curing salt is Morton Tender Quick. If 5 pounds seems like a little much for your first try, don't hesitate to cut the recipe in half because it will turn out just fine. After baking the rolls of salami it will freeze well, wrap tightly.

Courtesy Blake Miller – Outdoor Quest – www.outdoorquest.biz

EASY DUTCH OVEN APPLE COBBLER

Crumb Cake Mix
16-20oz Apples (canned or fresh)
10oz Sprite
Butter
Vanilla Ice Cream (or Whipped Cream)

Spray the Dutch oven with non-stick cooking spray. Cover the bottom of the oven with half of the cake mix. Pour in 1 oz of Sprite evenly over cake mix. Pour in contents of apple cans. Pour in the rest of the contents of the cake mix. Pour in 9 oz of soda evenly over the cake mix. Slice chunks of butter on top of cobbler. Cover the Dutch oven. Use 10 hot briquettes beneath. Put 16-20 briquettes on the lid. Cooking will take 45 to 60 minutes.

Steve McGrath, Camp Chef, www.campchef.com

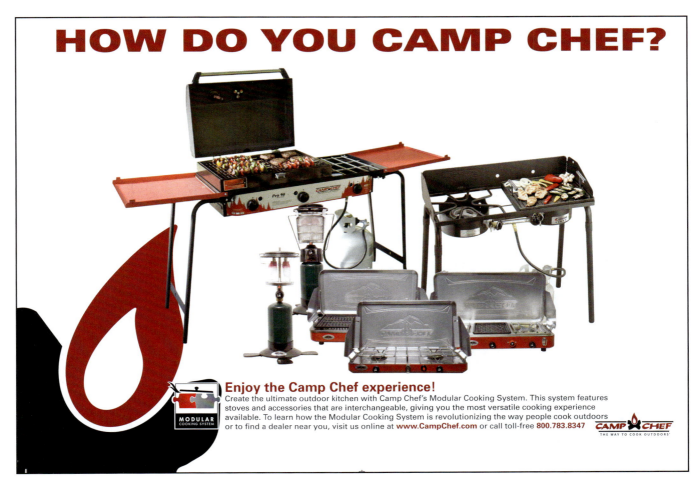

PASSING IT ON

If you've ever wondered when is the right time to introduce a young person to the world of hunting, you're not alone. Most hunters who are parents have asked themselves the same question.

Oregon offers big game hunts designed for kids aged 12-17. A 'First Time' hunt program guarantees that youngsters will be eligible to receive up to three tags: one for buck deer, one for antlerless deer and one for antlerless elk. See the Big Game Regulations.

There is no minimum age to hunt small game. If a child can pass Hunter Ed, they can hunt rabbits, ground squirrels and birds. To hunt big game, a hunter must be at least 12 years old, unless they are enrolled in Oregon's new Mentored Youth Hunter Program. The MYHP allows youth between the ages of 9 and 13 to hunt while supervised by a licensed adult. Only one firearm or bow may be carried between the two hunters.

Ask for *Hunting Oregon* at:
Fisherman's Marine - Coyote Ranch Pub - Borders
Cent-Wise Sporting Goods - Barnes and Noble
Shooters Pro Shop - Great Basin Sporting Goods
and other fine stores...

Hunting serves to widen a child's wealth of experience. Target shooting and the hunt help a youngster to focus, pay attention to detail and to better appreciate the natural world and their place in it.

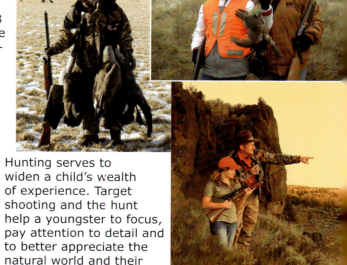

Oregon Department of Fish and Wildlife

Headquarters
3406 Cherry Avenue NE
Salem, OR 97303-4924
503-947-6000
800-720-6339

Controlled Hunts
503-947-6102
800-708-1782
www.dfw.state.or.us

Regional Offices

High Desert
61374 Parrell Road
Bend, OR 97702
541-388-6363

Northeast
107 20th Street
La Grande, OR 97850
541-963-2138

Northwest
17330 SE Evelyn Street
Clackamas, OR 97015
971-673-6000

Southwest
4192 N. Umpqua Hwy
Roseburg, OR 97470
541-440-3353

Local Offices

www.dfw.state.or.us/agency/directory/local_offices.asp

Map Sources

Bend Mapping
541-389-7440
www.bendmapping.com

Delorme
207-846-7000
www.delorme.com

MyTopo
877-587-9004
www.mytopo.com

Associations

Central Oregon Shooting Sports Association
www.oregonshooting.com

Ducks Unlimited
www.ducksunlimited.org

Metolius River Association –lodging, recreation, events
www.metoliusriver.com

Mule Deer Foundation
www.muledeer.org

National Rifle Association
www.nra.org

National Shooting Sports Foundation
www.nssf.org

National Wild Turkey Federation
www.nwtf.org

Oregon Bow Hunters
www.oregonbowhunters.com

Oregon Hunters Association
www.oregonhunters.org

Pheasants Forever
www.pheasantsforever.com

Quail Unlimited
www.qu.org

Rocky Mountain Elk Foundation
www.rmef.org

Ruffed Grouse Society
www.ruffedgrousesociety.org

Safari Club International
www.scifirstforhunters.org

U.S. Sportsmen's Alliance
www.ussafoundation.org

**To report wildlife violations, call
800-452-7888**

INDEX OF ADVERTISERS

Alder Creek Ranch	14
Alpen Optics	106
Animal Emergency Center	16
Annie's Healing Hearts	13
Bama's Wildlife Reflections	118
Bar-Lee Setters	31
Battle Creek Outfitters	81
Big K Guest Ranch	34
Black Oak Outfitters	74
Cabin Creek Kennels	20
Camp Chef	125
Cascade Bad Boy Buggies	67
Central Oregon Sporting Clays	32
Central Oregon Sporting Dogs	17
Coyote Ranch	56
Coyote Ranch Pub	44
Deep Canyon Preserve	21
Dennis Turmon Enterprises, LLC	100
Diamond-A Guides	113
FlySpur Ranch	70
Gary Lewis Outdoors	72, 117, 126
Great Basin Sporting Goods	48
GunTraders	76
Haugen Enterprises	62
Herzcoff Kennels	24
High Life PudelPointers	30
Holland's Shooter Supply	90
Horse Plaza	73
Horse Ridge Pistoleros	37
Jody Smith's Guide Service	62
Justin Latham Excavation, Inc.	11
Kootenai Valley Inflatables	8
Lake in the Dunes	28
Leavitt's	76
Les Schwab Tires	Inside Front Cover
Longhorn Lumber Co.	58
McLagan's Taxidermy	116
Nosler	86
NW Eco Mulching and Mowing	78
Old Rattler Productions	100
Olex Hunting Preserve	29
Oregon Department of Fish and Wildlife	114
Oregon Horse Packing	71
Oregon Hunters Association	119
Oregon Tag Guide	120
Orion's Choice	15
Orvis	12
Outdoor Quest	113
Patented Game Winch	82
Phoenix Asphalt	124
Pine Country Outfitters	27
Raymond James and Associates, LLC	79
Rocking L Log Homes	68
Rocky Mountain Elk Ranch	108
Rocky Ridge Hunting Club	92
Roe Outfitters	9
Service Creek Lodge	89
Shur-Cure	99
Snow's Transmissions	65
SportHill	88
Stormy Weather Kennels	19
SunSpots Safaris	64
SwiftCreek Elements	67
TecLabs, Inc.	25
Top Pin Archery Pro Shop	Inside Back Cover
Wallowa Lake Vacation Rentals	83
Warne Scope Mounts	111
Wild Winds Ranch	23
Wilderness Unlimited	69
Wolf Custom Painting	26
Wooster Design Inspirations	36
Youth Outdoor Adventures	110